EXPERIENCING
ORGANIZATIONS

EXPERIENCING ORGANIZATIONS

Stephen Fineman
and
Yiannis Gabriel

SAGE Publications
London · Thousand Oaks · New Delhi

This edition first published in 1996

SAGE Publications Ltd
6 Bonhill Street
London EC2A 4PU

SAGE Publications Inc
2455 Teller Road
Thousand Oaks, California 91320

SAGE Publications India Pvt Ltd
32, M-Block Market
Greater Kailash - I
New Delhi 110 048

British Library Cataloguing in Publication data

A catalogue record for this book is
available from the British Library

ISBN 0 8039 7870-7
ISBN 0 8039 7871-5 (pbk)

Library of Congress catalog record available

Typeset by Type Study, Scarborough, North Yorkshire
Printed in Great Britain at the University Press, Cambridge

Contents

Acknowledgements

This book could not have happened without the insights and perceptiveness of our students of Business Administration at the University of Bath's School of Management, during the years 1993–95. Their fascinating experiences stimulated the writing of the book, and provided a large measure of its content. We are also indebted to Sue Jones of Sage Publications whose support for our project has been consistent and enthusiastic.

Introduction

The tales told by new entrants to organizations are revealing. Their experiences of work are fresh and sharp; they will 'see' what older hands no longer notice or care about. An articulate, critical, but naïve worker can offer poignant insights on the rights and wrongs of organizational life – its passions, performances and pretences. As such, they open a window offering an unusual view of organizations, a view which is especially engaging for those who are studying working life, to whom this book is primarily addressed. Compared to conventional case studies, stories offer a different and particularly interesting way of examining and analysing personal experiences.

This book brings together a collection of stories about life in organizations, reported by a group of new organizational recruits. Their accounts followed six-month periods of paid work – an integral part of their studies at university. As slices of organizational life, these accounts offer two things. First, a vivid and immediate sense of what organizational roles, relationships and politics look and feel like at the turn of the new century. Secondly, in contrast to the rigid categories of traditional textbooks, they spotlight significant, if transient, moments in organizational life, presented with passion and authenticity.

Learning from Stories

There are many different ways in which we convey experiences of, and learn about, work life. Telling stories is one of them. Exchanging gossip, jokes and anecdotes is often central to the way we make sense of our experiences. This process goes on incessantly in workplace corridors, offices and coffee-rooms, and continues at home in accounts of 'what happened at work today'.

In some social sciences, especially anthropology and ethnography, stories are taken very seriously.[1, 2] This approach has recently been adopted in the study of organizations. Stories are an important ingredient of an organization's culture; they express personal and organizational meanings and feelings, especially in terms of the metaphors people use.[3, 4] Stories can tell something of the myths that an organization preserves, along with its heroes and heroines, and deeper-seated conflicts and anxieties.[5, 6] Finally, story-sharing can be therapeutic – a safety-valve for discontent or a route to improving an organization and its working relationships.[7, 8]

In short, we can regard stories as expressions of how people 'naturally' code their feelings, experiences and cultural expectations. Stories are a rich mixture of the storyteller's needs and wishes, as well as his or her reconstructions for a particular audience. The truth, or truths, of each story lie not in its accuracy but in its meanings, since stories are reproductions of lived realities rather than objective descriptions of 'facts'.

Each story can be read broadly as an indicator of what the teller remembers and thinks worth recounting. Different people may respond differently to the same story, focusing on contrasting details and varied emotional nuances. It is certainly a sign of a good story if people identify many levels of significance. Yet, stories can also be analysed more systematically and decoded for their subtexts and hidden meanings – what particular words, phrases and details suggest about the qualities of working life and the storyteller's sensibilities.

The Storytellers and their Accounts

The young people, whose stories we reproduce, had little or no formal work experience – it was their first rendezvous with 'proper' work. All entered their placement (internship) organizations relatively open-eyed and unjaundiced, carrying with them just a little formal learning in organizational behaviour.

The trainees worked for corporations in the public and private sectors, in service and manufacturing organizations, in large enterprises and small ones. Most of these organizations were located in the United Kingdom, though some were in other countries – Germany, Norway, Greece, Hong Kong and the United States. Just under half of the stories are told by non-British people.

Shortly after returning from their placements, as part of the debriefing process, they were asked by us to report on their experiences, as follows:

Please think of the organization in which you did your placement. What was it like? Try to recall an incident or conversation which captures or symbolizes what working for that organization was all about. Describe and discuss such an incident, something that taught you a lot about the organization, its management, its employees and its culture. Discuss your emotions at the time of the incident and now, as you look back at it.

In this book we report almost verbatim, and with the tellers' permission, some forty-five of their stories. The identities of the respondents, the companies, and all personnel, are disguised. The accounts represent the key themes evident in a total pool of over 400 stories. Each story was selected on the grounds that it seemed to us to have something important to say, and to be saying it in an informative and engaging manner. Together, the selected stories represent the range of issues expressed. Initially, the stories were identified and classified according to key 'messages' or 'morals' they communicated, the emotions expressed, the main actors involved, and the type and sector of the organization. In compiling our material, we grouped three or four stories in chapters sharing a common theme. We then arranged these chapters under three broad headings, each covered in a separate part of the book:

1 *Images*   The chapters in this section underline the trainees' realizations that appearances in organizations are often deceptive, and realities multi-layered. Many organizational roles and events are seen as 'staged' and the trainees attempt to read special meanings into them.
2 *Winning and Losing*   This section approaches organizations as structures of overlapping games, with groups and individuals competing for resources, power and recognition. Participants observe these games and try to understand their rules, as well as the tactics and strategies of different players.
3 *Survival and Injuries*   These chapters describe the wounds and bruises caused by some organizational encounters. Trainees reflect on ways people cope, and how they survive the difficulties and hardships of organizational life.

There is considerable overlap across the parts and chapters of the book. It is a characteristic of stories that their themes, details, emotional content and moral messages are not neatly compartmentalized or continuous. Our attempt to organize the material has produced by no means the only sequence possible, and the reader may well seek, and find, other connections and juxtapositions.

We have provided a short commentary to each story, drawing the reader's attention to some of the main themes, qualities and meanings that we feel are of interest. Our own backgrounds in organizational behaviour, psychology and sociology obviously colour what we 'see'. In this we are clearly influenced by our particular perspectives on life in organizations – which are broadly 'social constructionist' and 'psychodynamic'. We believe that social life and social order are very much interpretive; they depend on how actors experience and perceive their worlds and the kinds of formal and informal ways they negotiate, and adapt to, their interpersonal relationships. This can be conflictual or collaborative, smooth or painful, involving personal preferences and concerns – some carried unconsciously. The mobilization of politics and power is an inextricable part of these processes, and the particulars of each organization – its history, culture, rules and technologies – further shape work meanings and personal experiences.

A large number of the accounts which follow have an intimate, confessional quality, as respondents reveal things which they suspect they were not meant to witness. Their status as temporary workers afforded many of them an opportunity to hear and see things that permanent staff cannot witness directly. Some of the stories are comic, others traumatic or even epic, encompassing a broad range of emotions – joy, despair, frustration, pride, anxiety, fear, relief, amusement.

Another characteristic is the distance between the public images of famous companies as portrayed in their advertisements, public relations literature and press reports, and the often messy, confused and down-beat reality experienced once inside. For many of the trainees, their first encounter with corporate life was one of disappointment or dismay. They tell of their disenchantment and new-found suspicion of the 'challenge' and 'achievement' of managerial work. They also express a loss of innocence, reflecting on the naïve assumptions they had entertained before being exposed to the 'real world'.

We make no claim that the pictures which unfold in this book are statistically representative of all possible shades of work experience. They present just one phase of work-encounter in the form of a series of intense snapshots – where the new recruits hold the camera. It must be born in mind that the pictures were meant for a particular audience: their university lecturers. The result, however, is a composite portrait of a particular group of people 'working' their uncertain identities, potential and idealism, and becoming more streetwise.

This overall picture has a further facet worthy of mention: it offers a suggestive portrait of organizational life at a particular point in history. It was a time when organizational downsizing, re-engineering and restructuring became part of the new managerial ethic, with massive technological changes in some industries. The cold realities for many people in mid or late career included unemployment, job insecurity, retraining or early retirement. For younger people entering the workforce, competition for available posts at all levels was fierce. It was a testing era for equal opportunities in British employment practices, particularly with regard to women at work. Sackings, discrimination, departmental closures, rationalizations, intrigues and insecurity all feature prominently in this book. Organizations do not appear as especially integrated units, in which different parts work harmoniously; nor do not they emerge as particularly pleasant or ethical places in which to work.

There are reasons why our respondents' accounts may over-accentuate the negative. Disappointed idealism, premature cynicism and the critical qualities encouraged by universities may all conspire in a bleak presentation of organizations. Nevertheless, it seems to us that many of the stories capture something of the harsher realities of organizational life after more than a decade of insecurity and retrenchment.

Using this Book

We feel that this book makes fascinating reading in its own right, and we invite readers to taste some of the oddities, plots and suspense of working life, conveyed in literary-style presentation. The material generated by new job entrants has a face validity and plausibility which is readily accessible to students of organizational behaviour and management. Importantly, it shows to new learners something of the complexity of 'real' work experiences, while sensitizing them to different ways of understanding organizational activities.

The book is a valuable companion to more traditional, concept-driven, textbooks and to conventional case studies. It offers rich, multidimensional 'happenings' for analysis, and brings new learners closer to what may be their own experience of working. It also helps in the questioning of the more simplistic recipes and theories of action and performance. In our own activities as lecturers we have found some of the stories contained in this book highly stimulating for class discussion, both in small and larger groups. The lecturer may wish to encourage students to focus their analysis on the particular content-area of an ongoing teaching programme. For example, we have found issues of gender, emotions, power, politics, motivation, stress, bureaucracy and change are vividly brought to life in the accounts. Analyses can be written as formal pieces of work in response to specific questions posed by the instructor. Additionally, many of the stories have a 'so what?' quality; they invite the reader to reflect on what went wrong, how he or she would have acted in similar circumstances, and how things might work out in the future.

To encourage such reflection we have added a number of questions at the end of each chapter, specific to the stories of the chapter (Thinking On). There are no correct answers to these questions, though some are better than others. Readers, especially instructors, may wish to add their own questions to ours. Each chapter concludes with a bibliographical section (Reading On). These are not meant to be exhaustive, though we have tried to bring to the reader's attention sources which are both important and not entirely 'obvious'.

Reading On

There are some introductory texts which make good companions for the present book:

Boje, D.M. and Dennehy, R.F. (1993). *Managing in the Postmodern World*. Dubuque, IA: Kendall-Hunt.

Frost, P.J., Mitchell, V.F. and Nord, W.R. (eds) (1992). *Organizational Reality: Reports from the Firing Line* (4th edn). New York: HarperCollins.

Handy, C.B. (1976). *Understanding Organizations*. Harmondsworth: Penguin.

Hellriegel, D., Slocum, J.W. and Woodman, R.W. (1995). *Organizational Behavior*. Minneapolis/St Paul, MN: West.

Hucynski, A. and Buchanan, D. (1985). *Organisational Behaviour*. New York: Prentice Hall.

Ritti, R.R. and Funkhouser, G.R. (1977). *The Ropes to Skip and the Ropes to Know: Studies In Organizational Behaviour*. Columbus, OH: Grid Publishing.

Sims, D., Fineman, S. and Gabriel, Y. (1993). *Organizing and Organizations: An Introduction*. London: Sage.

Notes

1 Boje, M. (1991). 'The storytelling organization: a study of story performance in an office-supply firm', *Administrative Science Quarterly*, 36, 106–26.

2 Martin, J. (1992). 'Stories and scripts in organizational settings', in A. Hastorf and A. Isen (eds), *Cognitive Social Psychology*. New York: Elsevier-North Holland.

3 Feldman, M.S. (1991). 'The meanings of ambiguity; learning from stories and metaphors', in P.J. Frost, L.F. Moore, M.R. Louis, C.C. Lundberg and J. Martin (eds), *Reframing Organizational Culture*. Newbury Park, CA: Sage.

4 Brown, A. (1995). *Organisational Culture*. London: Pitman.

5 Gabriel, Y. (1991). 'Turning facts into stories and stories into facts: a hermeneutic exploration of organizational folklore', *Human Relations*, 44, 8, 857–75.

6 Hansen, C.D. and Kahnweiler, W. M. (1993). 'Storytelling: an instrument for understanding the dynamics of corporate relationships', *Human Relations*, 46, 12, 1391–409.

7 Reason, P. and Hawkins, P. (1988). 'Storytelling as inquiry', in P. Reason (ed.), *Human Inquiry in Action*. London: Sage.

8 Akin, G. and Schultheiss, E. (1990). 'Jazz bands and missionaries: OD through stories and metaphor', *Journal of Managerial Psychology*, 5, 4, 12–18.

PART 1
IMAGES

Ours is an image-conscious era. We are surrounded by images of objects, of people, of organizations. We are also highly aware of our own images, especially those we choose to display to others. Many of us devote time and money to perfecting them. We look at ourselves in mirrors, photographs or on TV screens; we try out different styles and purchase different image-enhancing products, such as clothes, cars and make-up.

By combining different ingredients, we may seek to create images that are original, exciting and appealing. We smile a lot, trying to appear friendly, or we adopt deliberately affected airs trying to look cool. We power-dress when we go to critical meetings, or we dress casually when we want to appear relaxed. Dressing casually does not mean that we wear the first set of clothes that we find; casualness usually requires a lot of thought. Images and appearances are products of artifice; yet, they are vital in the way we conceive and construct reality. We constantly rely on them for judging people, objects and organizations.

Living in an image-conscious world means that we also cultivate deep suspicions. An image may be accurate or phoney; it may conceal hidden depths or it may be nothing more than a shining surface. We may be mistrustful of glamorous images, fearing that behind attractive appearances, realities will be different. So we continuously explore and test images, looking for clues about what they may conceal.

Organizations are themselves enmeshed in different images, like those of rationality, power and order. Words like 'excellence', 'quality' and 'customer service', corporate slogans and logos, gleaming corporate headquarters, expensive furnishings and high salaries all contribute to our picture of organizations. Some such images are easily punctured. They are but a facade, a 'public relations' exercise, bearing little relation to the organizational realities as experienced by their members. There are times, however, when organizations will make enormous efforts and sacrifices in order to live up to these images. A 'caring' firm, for example, may find itself torn between its 'no redundancies' policy and the need to cut costs. A company which claims that 'the customer is always right' may find itself sorely tested by awkward or dishonest customers intent on taking advantage of it.

It is not surprising, then, to find that a large number of stories told by new organizational recruits focus on this subject. Some muse over the gap between the initial images they had of the organization and the reality they encountered. Others choose to highlight the difference between the world of organizations which they mastered through their textbooks and lecture programmes – rational, organized, transparent – and the messiness and chaos of much of everyday organizational life. There are those who are highly aware of the images they themselves are projecting to their colleagues and superiors as members of work organizations; they contrast them to the images which they adopt outside such organizations. Yet others concentrate on the ways particular colleagues or leaders present themselves. Are they being genuine, or not?

It can be upsetting to penetrate someone's facade. If an idealized image suddenly collapses, what might be left? In the stories that follow, some of the trainees come to regard such a happening as the end of innocence and credulity. Others view it as a rite of passage and are proud to have conquered their earlier *naïveté*.

1

Images and Mirages

Organizations seem solid – solid buildings, solid people, solid products, solid money. Many of them are shining too, at least if we judge them from the glamour of their brochures, the opulence of their buildings, the aura of their logos and the sheen of their products.

The mental images of organizations carried by some young people when they go for their job interviews can be highly idealized. Yet, reading through their accounts of their actual work experiences, we are struck by how quickly the appearance of solidity and the appeal can evaporate. New recruits are left surprised at their own gullibility. Was what they imagined the organization to be nothing but a mirage, a carefully presented image? Is the reality really confusion and pettiness?

The first story, told by Pierre, a French student, is about the serious shattering of illusions, precipitated by a small event.

Pierre's Story: A Holy Place!

The incident I am going to describe took place in the first few weeks of my placement at the Plastics Division of REP, an American multinational. Two ladies from Customer Service were having a talk, at the desk opposite to me. Their jobs involve mediating between the customer and the computer system for orders and shipments. Although their jobs are essential to REP, they have a low status in REP's 'ranks'. As my work was a bit routine at that time, I decided to listen in on their conversation.

Their discussion started with a description of the previous managing director who had treated most of his workers, other than the managers and salespeople, as insignificant. As a result, managers had become conceited and arrogant, viewing lower-ranked employees as second-class citizens. One of their stories concerned an event in the car park, where a salesperson with a new company car made some disparaging remarks about the car of one of the two ladies having the conversation. From then on, the conversation switched towards the negative aspects of the sales-force, their arrogance about their cars, their treatment of others and how they took all the credit and recognition for good sales. The conversation evolved into a commentary on most of the employees at REP, especially on managers. A lot of nasty things were being said, so I decided to stop listening.

I felt that what I had heard was very revealing. Once in a while it is normal to hear people grumbling at each other, but this was much more serious. A lot of major criticisms were coming from these two ladies. This was the first time I heard major complaints and 'slandering'. The women were definitely letting out a lot of frustration and feelings about the way things were going on at REP.

It is important now to reveal that my father has worked for REP throughout his entire working life. He is now the Managing Director of its French subsidiary. Many of my old school friends have had parents working there, forming a small, close-knit community. To me and my friends, REP had been a holy place all through our lives, a place where people were really happy. How many times had I heard my father say, 'Why don't you work for REP, Pierre?' At my old school they used to call us 'REP kids'. REP was always a part of my life.

Until I heard this conversation, REP was still, in my eyes, a place where politics and negative emotions had no place. I know it is a very naïve approach, but I admit to seeing REP as a near perfect organization. I thought REP was like a team or family, just like my manager had told me at my first interview. The 'official' reputation of REP is of a company which is run like a team, where people help each other out.

This incident taught me that REP is not like its official facade, even though the new MD is trying to change things. There are strained relations between managers and their staff. I now see there are many small crises that occur in REP, which are not addressed. I now know to tread lightly within the organization. I do not want be treated like an arrogant student whose father is MD for REP France. I have learned to watch my step when I'm with other workers or managers. I never make any comments about people, and I resist taking sides. I've learned that everyone in the office is under close scrutiny.

At the time I felt betrayed. I had always been encouraged to see REP as an excellent organization, but the incident showed that this wasn't the case. This conversation shocked me; it made me quite angry. I also felt a sense of disbelief about the amount of resentment that existed in the company. I now feel frustrated, because I think something should be done about the problems raised by the two ladies having the conversation. I also feel stupid when I realize I was so naïve about REP's state. I see this whole event as having two morals. The first is not to believe an organization's official reputation. The second is to 'lie low', never take sides, and keep your nose clean.

It took nothing more than an overheard conversation between two ordinary members of staff to shake Pierre's faith in REP. The idealized image of the company was not one lifted from corporate brochures and rhetoric, but one nurtured by countless homilies by his father. This picture was supported by the taken-for-granted status of REP among Pierre's close friends and their parents. Why should Pierre not believe in the goodness of REP?

In many respects this story resonates with the ambivalent feelings between father and son, and the father's career aspirations for his son. Pierre does not accuse his father of *deliberately* deceiving him but, as he loses faith in the company, he seems to lose faith in previously trusted authorities and, to some extent, in himself. His sense of betrayal is not directed at the two women who were bad-mouthing the organization he had grown up to regard as a 'holy place', but those with whom he had colluded in sustaining this image.

Is his reaction a bit exaggerated? Is betrayal too strong a word to describe his feelings? We think not. His account is a classic story centring on the theme of the end of innocence. Pierre 'feeling stupid' about his *naïveté* is not very different from the feelings of children who finally accept that Father Christmas does not exist, long after they have suspected the truth.

The first of the two morals which Pierre reads into the story is a valuable lesson; organizations should not be judged by their official reputations, any more than books should be judged by their covers. Growing up means learning to question some of the idealized images bequeathed to us by well-meaning, though over-protective, others. There is always something sad about leaving this innocent idealism behind, and most of us seek to redirect at least some of it onto new objects, lovers, children, projects and missions. The child in us may then continue to live side-by-side, rather than in conflict, with our more mature selves.

The second moral drawn by Pierre – that he must always keep a low profile in order not to be judged – can become a double-edged sword, either a valuable lesson or a debilitating affliction. It seems right that he should be cautious before expressing views which may be hurtful or demeaning to others; it is less desirable that he should become an organizational chameleon, without views and opinions of his own, mistrustful of everyone. The demise of early idealism should not be replaced, or overcompensated for, by overbearing cynicism and suspicion.

Discovering that a company is not all that it is purported to be is not always an unpleasant experience, especially if the organization can then become a target for laughter and amusement. This is illustrated in the second story, narrated by Mark, who worked for a company of steel stockholders in the West of England.

Mark's Story: When Theories Encounter Reality

The first week of my placement was spent at CUS's Head Office in Bradford, where I received training on how to install and run a new computerized budget system. It was designed to streamline information gathering. This training consisted of one afternoon and a fault-plagued demonstration. I returned to CUS Yeovil marginally wiser, with a promise that the software would arrive early the following week.

A full fortnight later we received the package to install in all the south-western units. This was first done at my unit in Yeovil. My manager and I then set off for Bodmin and Cardiff to repeat the exercise. During the journey, our sales manager telephoned to tell us that the data produced by the new system were all wrong. We contacted Head Office and it was discovered that the entire download from the company mainframe was corrupt.

We continued on our journey, planning simply to install the database software (appropriately named Paradox) needed to run the system, without downloading the data. On arrival at Bodmin we found that their A4 printer was unable to produce the necessary A3 reports and at Cardiff their PC could not cope with the program. New problems on top of old ones.

After several unsuccessful attempts, we managed to install the system on the machines. But the problems kept piling up. Unfortunately, Bradford had issued only minimal instructions on how to use the system and were expecting ridiculous degrees of accuracy. No training sessions were offered. This left sales staff confused and often angry, swearing alternately at Head Office and the computers. Numerous bugs continued to lurk in the system. Unsurprisingly we failed to meet the deadline for going 'live' on the system, and the system failed to impress anyone forced to operate it. Thereafter things went from bad to worse.

This incident, happening as it did at the very start of my placement, was like being doused with icy water. Such corporate confusion! Where was the efficient bureaucracy? What had happened to the clear communications networks? Hadn't they ever heard of team management? In short, why was there so little evidence of the neat formal theories we learned in our university courses? It could not be a matter of education, for the Marketing Department was wholly made up of graduates. I started to think and to question.

As I was running around trying to keep the leaky system afloat, I chatted with many unit and sales managers. The idea behind the new information system was essentially a good one, but it simply didn't work in practice. Instead of reducing the work done by units it increased it. And often I heard the words '. . . but I want it to do this . . .' or '. . . but I don't need to know that!'

Gradually, I came to the conclusion that the problems lay with the Marketing Department, or more precisely the assumptions made by its staff. Indeed, it wasn't until this chaotic series of events that I realized that most of us get trapped into a particular way of seeing the world. Although our personalities are often very different, we generally are of the same generation with similar ways of thinking. I would suggest that many of us stride boldly into the business world, confident that we can solve its problems with our battery of theory – only to find that bucket of cold reality waiting for us. In this instance, the whole Marketing Department was made up of such people.

I was able to watch from a different viewpoint as the Marketing Department pressed on from their own particular angle, confident in their theoretical grounding. Seeing how this grounding was swept away demonstrated to me the limitations of the 'textbook' approach. It has altered my perspective on how to use the knowledge from the lectures.

Many of the problems that arose could have been avoided with more common sense and better communications. I hope that incidents of this nature are rare within industry, but somehow I doubt it. Such episodes show that how outsiders may perceive, or be conditioned into perceiving, an organization can be very different from the reality. Certainly the 'Total Quality' image promoted by CUS is not reflected in this internal debacle.

To begin with I was confused. On top of the usual disorientation of a new environment I felt I had found quicksand where there should have been solid ground. As I sank into this, shock became distaste. Fortunately, my boss and I shared a dry wit and pragmatic attitude (he later resigned!). He encouraged me to learn from CUS's mistakes and take it as it came. Looking back now the incident is almost funny, a modern comedy of errors. But I feel that it would have been easy for a naïve student like myself to have emerged feeling disillusioned and cynical.

Mark's idealized image of organizations was not the product of parental and local-community influence (as was Pierre's), but rather of excessive respect for academic theory. He was not so much disillusioned with the company itself, as with the theories which seemed to fail him in his hour of need. Whatever happened to good theories when the organization was crying out for them? Interestingly, Mark's analysis of what went wrong hinges on the same factor, namely the inability of those who designed the new computer system to relate their technical ideas to the requirements of ordinary users. As graduates, they felt they could decide which system was best for the firm purely on its technical merits, disregarding stubborn organizational realities – like the habits and limitations of users, their accumulated knowledge, their likes and dislikes.

The organizational quicksand, which Mark vividly described, was frightening at the time; in hindsight, however, it seemed more like a comedy of errors. Disorder, disorganization and chaos are not threatening once they are accepted as part and parcel of organizational life, rather than as 'problems' which 'batteries of theory' can resolve. Mark is now older and wiser, or so he wishes to portray himself. He can laugh at the organization, at the lack of pragmatism of the graduates of the Marketing Department, and at his own excessive trust of theory. Yet, he is not totally ready to surrender his faith in theory, toying with the idea that better communication might have prevented the disaster.

So it is not theory, after all, which has failed the company, but the wrong choice of theory. In time, Mark may recognize that most theories in social sciences are not simple tools for fixing problems. Theories, especially the appropriate choice of a theory, may help us identify and define a problem, analyse its causes and perhaps mitigate its effects. To expect theory to do much beyond that, is to cast it in the role of faith.

Pierre's and Mark's stories, like many others in this book, highlight the discovery that there is a big gap between an organization's presented image and the students' own lived experiences of the same organization. Their tales reveal strong emotions about this, such as betrayal, shock, confusion and elation. The final story of this chapter does something different; it describes an organization, appropriately a prestigious jewellers', in which the image *is* the essence. Jane describes in detail, and somewhat satirically, the symbols which sustain the company's allure. She then relates an incident which tested this allure to breaking point.

Jane's Story: The Company Where Time Stands Still

The place: Church's, Jewellers, Silversmiths and Goldsmiths by appointment to Her Majesty the Queen, in New York's exclusive Fifth Avenue, where life, money and technology remain their same old selves. This prestigious shop sells jewellery as well as leather merchandise, semi-precious stone carvings and rare books. Nothing has changed at all except for the comings and goings of English students on placement, chosen for their English accents and good looks.

The time: Thursday 9 August established itself at 9.30 a.m. to be just another of those ordinary, unexciting – namely boring – days that I had already encountered for my first two weeks there. But by 3 p.m. the store was in turmoil. Yes, 'it' had finally happened in the store where plastic is only ever seen in the shape of gold and platinum credit cards, where the clientele are treated impeccably and where no more than two pieces of jewellery are allowed out of a showcase at once. What happened? The abduction of a beautiful and stunningly rich bracelet.

The revolving door swirled around and a youngish-looking gentleman dressed in a smart suit entered the store. Everyone automatically glanced up for a second, then resumed their duties. He wandered around, casually gazing at the rock crystal obelisk and admiring the $1 million semi-precious stone elephant, which had been the shop's glorious centrepiece for over two and a half years. Those normally gullible enough to purchase such items had shown a lack of interest.

After being pointed to the stairs that led to the jewellery section, he sauntered across, and with an air of richness that was too rich to be rich, he ascended. From the other sales assistant, who was meant to be watching the proceedings, we learnt that the gentleman was interested in bracelets 'for a lady friend'.

The strange aura of 'coolness' that surrounded the client had been enough to arouse the suspicion of one of the students, who reported him to security. This should have led to a prompt increase of security upstairs, but as I have already said 'Church's stands still', and that is what happened – it was noted and forgotten.

The gentleman upstairs seemed infatuated with the bracelet that was paved with diamonds, centred with a sapphire as big as your thumb nail, and set in 18K yellow gold. He was comparing it with another bracelet, of not such a high price.

Then he noticed the newly-commissioned 'Deer Necklace', and as the sales assistant turned momentarily to gaze at it, he whipped the expensive bracelet into his pocket, thanked the lady for assistance, and was descending the stairs before she could blink. The problem, of course, was that neither she nor anyone else actually saw the gentleman take it. Without a proper sighting of the theft, he was allowed to walk out of the store $25,000 richer, the option of searching him denied to the security staff.

Church's now buzzed with the news and tears of annoyance, anger and disbelief could be heard from the President's Office. The sales assistant emerged 20 minutes later, red-faced and puffy-eyed and promptly left. The whole 'hush-hush' occurrence lasted for about half an hour, and apart from a single policeman who arrived for a statement, no one would have known that anything at all had taken place. No reporters, no roping-off areas, nothing.

Church's once again lived up to itself. Of course, the President was deeply upset, and said so at the meeting at the end of the day. 'Increase security,' he said, 'be careful, always be on the alert, watch everyone – everyone is a potential thief. No matter how rich or poor, remember it is usually the very rich who steal because they cannot bear to part with their money.' He continued, 'Oh, well done', to the student who reported him, 'you could have emphasized your concern more . . . !' We all agreed, nodded in agreement, and left to enjoy an evening of drinking, eating and pool playing.

For about three days security was stepped up and everyone was on constant alert. But as time went on, the store became relaxed and returned to its original self. Church's did not want to change, and even an occurrence like this did not push them forward. Although, when we were robbed again two weeks later of a $3,000 book, they did take one step forward to look at themselves, then promptly took two steps backwards again.

The image of traditional English opulence in the midst of New York is one which obviously impressed Jane – just as it was meant to impress the 'clients' (such companies would not stoop to having 'customers'). Jane did not seek to lift the company's mask, as did Pierre and Mark; rather, she showed how a thief took advantage of the company's determination to treat its customers with dignity – to be consistent with its own rhetoric. Perhaps $25,000 may not be too high a price to pay for this!

'Everyone is a potential thief' is not a message which goes down well in a company determined to treat its clientele as it does its royal patrons. It is hard to imagine the Prince of Wales or the Sultan of Brunei being regarded as 'potential thieves', as per the exhortations of the president. It is perhaps asking too much of staff for them to be vigilant and suspicious, while providing the lofty service on which the company prides itself.

British students are selected by the company and flown 6,000 miles, not for their vigilance or business wits, but for their 'Englishness'. They are an integral part of an image, designed to appeal to American consumers of expensive jewellery. It can be demanding being part of a corporate image – as a shop assistant at a prestigious jewellers', an airline cabin attendant or a receptionist. Staff feel that they are constantly on display, whether the image is merely a veneer or, as in this story, a fairly accurate reflection of the company's heritage and values. The ironic twist in the story is that one of the 'decorative' students was alert enough to suspect the thief, while the security staff did nothing about it (probably dismissing her warning as excessive zeal on the part of an excitable student).

In the first two stories new organizational recruits are confronted with realities which fail to live up to expectations. The third story has all the amusing qualities of a stereotype reinforced; a company fully living up to its image. It is interesting that both CUS and REP, in spite of our students' disappointments, are highly successful and profitable companies. However, Church's American venture has not prospered, losing money year in, year out. Its poor performance has not been due to 'stock shrinkage', through incidents like the one described by Jane, or the high insurance premiums incurred. Its formula, it seems, has failed to captivate the American market. Its image may be bright, but not one which encourages clients to present their plastic gold often enough. Neither the glimmering image, nor a company's determination to live up to it, are by themselves recipes for success.

Thinking On

1   Companies employ firms of consultants and spend vast amounts of money refining their image. What are the processes and the signs through which a company's image is communicated to its own workforce, prospective employees, the public at large or the 'financial community'?
2   Why have young people, like our students, such idealized images of companies? What needs do such idealized images fulfil?
3   Is Pierre right to believe what the two women, whose conversation he overheard, said? Why does he not go into greater detail on what exactly they were saying that he found so shattering?
4   Some people enjoy working in highly organized environments; others prosper in conditions of chaos and disorder. Can the same be said about business organizations? How is it that CUS, which in Mark's eyes gets tangled up in comedies of errors, remains a highly successful company?
5   Can you take a guess as to why Church's marketing recipe, which works well in London and Kuala Lumpur, seems less successful in New York? What information would you require in order to assess whether Church's need to reconsider their entire marketing strategy?

Reading On

The gap between organizations as experienced by those working and living in them, and as portrayed by academic literature, is explored by Ritti and Funkhauser (1993) and Frost et al. (1992), whose collections try to illustrate the complexity, variety and unpredictability of organizational life. Two textbooks, by Boje and Dennehy (1993) and by Sims et al. (1993), try in different ways to provide portraits of organizations rooted in the experiences of their participants rather than deriving from academic theories. Both make extensive use of storytelling as a learning device. The authors of this book have discussed extensively the differences between traditional and alternative organizational textbooks (Fineman and Gabriel 1994).

Gagliardi (1990) has examined the way that material artifacts of an organization become symbols, reflecting the organization's image. Schein (1985) has studied the links between artifacts and symbols and deeper cultural processes in organizations; he has also examined the extent to which organizational cultures are internalized or resisted by new organizational recruits, developing a theory of organizational socialization (1988). Of considerable interest is Schwartz's work (1987, 1990) which describes how an organization's might and glamour can become part of its members' sense of self-identity; Schwartz has also shown how obsession with image can get in the way of achieving an organization's objectives.

More generally, the role of images in contemporary culture has been explored by numerous authors, especially in the area of consumption, where the success of a brand often depends on creating the right image. Notable contributions in this area have been made by Lasch (1980), Baudrillard (1988), Bourdieu (1984) and McCracken (1988). However, the importance of physical appearance and other attributes (accent, clothes, facial expressions, etc.) as part of the image a company seeks to project has been explored by Hochschild (1983) and several contributors in collections edited by Hearn et al. (1989) and Fineman (1993).

The theme of the end of innocence which accompanies the transition from childhood to adulthood lies at the centre of Robert Bly's (1990) book, *Iron John*. Baum (1987), Hirschhorn (1988) and Hopfl (1992) have discussed the cynicism that can result from a young person's first exposure to organizational politics.

Baudrillard, Jean (1988). *Selected Writings*, ed. Mark Poster. Cambridge: Polity Press.

Baum, H.S. (1987). *The Invisible Bureaucracy*. Oxford: Oxford University Press.

Bly, Robert (1990). *Iron John: A Book About Men*. New York: Addison-Wesley.

Boje, D.M. and Dennehy, R.F. (1993). *Managing in the Postmodern World: America's Revolution Against Exploitation*. Dubuque, IO: Kendall-Hunt.

Bourdieu, Pierre (1984). *Distinction: A Social Critique of the Judgement of Taste*. London: Routledge.

Fineman, S. (ed.) (1993). *Emotion in Organizations*. London: Sage.

Fineman, S. and Gabriel, Y. (1994). 'Paradigms of organizations: an exploration of textbook rhetorics', *Organization*, 1, 2, 375–99.

Frost, P.J., Mitchell, V.F. and Nord, W.R. (eds) (1992). *Organizational Reality: Reports from the Firing Line* (4th edn). New York: HarperCollins.

Gagliardi, Pasquale (1990). *Symbols and Artifacts: View of the Corporate Landscape*. New York: de Gruyter.

Hearn, J., Sheppard, D.L., Tancred-Sheriff, P. and Burrell, G. (eds) (1989). *The Sexuality of Organization*. London: Sage.

Hirschhorn, L. (1988). *The Workplace Within*. Cambridge, MA: MIT Press.

Hochschild, A. (1983). *The Managed Heart*. Berkeley, CA: University of California.

Hopfl, H. (1992). 'The making of the corporate acolyte', *Journal of Management Studies*, 29, 1, 23–34.

Lasch, C. (1980). *The Culture of Narcissism*. London: Abacus.

McCracken, Grant (1988). *Culture and Consumption: New Approaches to the Symbolic Character of Consumer Goods and Activities*. Bloomington, IN: Indiana University Press.

Ritti, R.R. and Funkhouser, G.R. (1993). *The Ropes to Skip and the Ropes to Know: Studies in Organizational Behaviour* (3rd edn). Columbus, OH: Grid Publishing.

Schein, E. (1985). *Organizational Culture and Leadership*. San Francisco, CA: Jossey-Bass.

Schein, E.H. (1988). 'Organizational socialization and the profession of management', *Sloan Management Review*, reprinted in Fall 1988, pp. 53–65 (original work published in 1968).

Schwartz, H.S. (1987). 'Anti-social actions of committed organizational participants: an existential psychoanalytic perspective', *Organization Studies*, 8, 4, 327–40.

Schwartz, H.S. (1990). *Narcissistic Process and Corporate Decay*. New York: New York University Press.

Sims, D., Fineman, S. and Gabriel, Y. (1993). *Organizing and Organizations: An Introduction*. London: Sage.

2

Performance and Impressions

Playing a part and creating the right impression is not something confined to the theatre. We take up roles on the organizational 'stage' and there are 'scripts' for different people in different circumstances – between bosses and subordinates, in job interviews and personnel appraisals, in committees and in corridors.

Performances are not just of the grand sort, such as when standing in front of an audience delivering a talk or lecture. They are part and parcel of all face-to-face encounters as we strive to present ourselves in ways that create certain impressions in the eyes of others; perhaps as authoritative and knowledgeable, caring and concerned, or in control of events. These impressions may or may not be how we feel or normally are, but they reflect what seems right for the situation. Performing, or presenting oneself, appropriately can be regarded as a skill necessary in all organizational encounters. Somehow, the new member of the organization has to learn acceptable mannerisms, dress and talk associated with his or her position or positions, and the leeway that is acceptable.

From this perspective, managing impressions is not to be seen as a false process, but one that is required for organizations to operate smoothly. It is an expression of our social selves and of the way we try to influence other people. Of course some roles will feel less comfortable than others. It can be stressful if we are called upon to don 'masks', or create images, that are significantly different from what we feel we are really like.

The importance of performance and impressions is highlighted in different ways in the following accounts from Paul, Dian and Nigel. Paul's, our first story, vividly depicts a telling event at a large public gathering of colleagues.

Paul's Story: *Faux pas*

The incident in question occurred during the annual Accountancy Students' Dinner Dance for all students in the area. The chap at the centre of the incident, Eric Minton, was an Oxbridge graduate recently appointed to the firm along with myself. These dinners are always attended by students who have yet to qualify as chartered accountants, and by senior management and partners. As is usual at these events it was 'open bar' and wine was flowing with the meal. One might forgive a man for getting rather loud and boisterous when drinking excessive quantities of alcohol, as Eric was. If things had stopped there nothing would have been remembered of the event.

It so happened that the invited guest speaker at this event was Jonathan Fox, the well-known TV Weatherman. He delivered a very entertaining and enjoyable speech which pleased Eric very much – he laughed and cheered. All pretty normal behaviour you may be thinking. At the end of Mr Fox's speech he asked his avid recipients if they had any questions that they would like to put to him. Eric, with an excited look similar to that of a nine-year-old school boy who knew the answer to teacher's very difficult maths question, thrust his hand into the air. Now Jonathan, who it has to be said was rather lacking in the hair department, looked across at Eric. Eric, in an eardrum-bursting voice, shouted: 'Jonathan, does the glowing sheen on the top of your head reflect the current economic climate?'

The room fell silent as 400 unamused accountants looked first at Eric and then Jonathan. The look on the faces of all the partners, students and senior management from the company said it all. It was then worsened by the fact that five seconds later Eric clapped his hands and laughed, with rather more gusto than was strictly necessary, at his very funny joke (as one imagines he supposed it to be).

Earlier in the evening we had all taken part in a sweepstake guessing how long Jonathan Fox's speech would last. Just after Eric's slight blunder one of the senior managers turned to me and said, 'the next sweepstake will be on how long Eric Minton will stay on the Branfeld's payroll'. It was said in jest but contained a strong element of threat.

This incident, although extreme, is a prime example of how everyone, in all aspects of life, is being judged in Branfeld – and the effect this has on their career. During the incident, I could not help the overwhelming feeling of embarrassment at our table, or for that matter the whole room. It was as if I was willing Eric to stop because I was realizing that, from this moment on, he will have been judged. People who have worked with Eric will lose respect for him, and people who have yet to work with him will have preconditioned ideas.

From the moment one enters Branfeld as an organization, every move you make is being observed, whether it be academic, in work, or social. I would liken it to being back at school. Academically you are being observed closely, penalized for failing exams, rewarded for passing. Failure can also result in being asked to leave the company. From the results of formative academic examinations, high-flyers are already being plucked out. Weekly judgements in the form of staff reports render this monitoring a constant aspect of one's position. These reports contain grading systems and a space for personal comments from seniors. This staff reporting-system is pay-related and continues all the way up the hierarchical structure.

In the incident above, Eric was being judged in the social aspects – as indeed we all were – at the dinner. I was sitting with partners either side of me. Hopefully I was being positively judged, unlike Eric, surely. During the incident, it was so obvious from the reactions of senior members of staff that his behaviour was not producing positive thoughts: 'Eric Minton is not fitting in to the Branfeld culture'. When a student's whole career within Branfeld balances upon their ability to 'fit in' to this culture, or way of life, one can see the importance of not breaking the mould.

At one level this story could be simply entitled 'Rather Drunk Employee Over-steps the Mark'. And indeed, this is exactly what Eric Minton unwittingly did. But what is clear, as the story unfolds, is that in observing Eric doing so Paul discovered exactly how important it is to maintain the 'correct' impressions.

The dinner dance had all the trappings of a relaxing social event, with alcohol and an amusing after-dinner speaker to enhance *bonhomie*. In any other gathering of this sort Eric Minton's remark may have drawn a nervous giggle, been ignored, booed or groaned at. Yet, what was immediately clear from the reaction, the setting was still essentially a *work* one, and one where proper organizational performances and roles could not be dispensed with. Minton's gaffe, failure to impress, or simply poor piece of clowning, was of considerable consequence. First to himself. He had failed to maintain sufficient propriety for a 'professional' accountant, albeit at a fun event (a good clown knows his or her limitations and 'reads' the audience well). Secondly, and no less consequentially, he had embarrassed 'his table' in full public view of students from other companies. This could dent reputations, perhaps not irrevocably, but sufficiently to make colleagues and superiors feel uncomfortable. We do not know of Minton's fate, but it is not untypical for such people to be used as scapegoats in companies who are anxious about their image.

Corporate socialization of new members can be rapid and powerful, to the extent that they soon learn the rules of how to present themselves – if they want to get on. Already, it seems, this process has taken a hold of Paul at an emotional level: *he* experienced the embarrassment that he wanted Minton to feel, wishing that the debacle would stop. This behaviour reflects the power of the organization's culture. It can breed anxiety and restrict creativity among those fearful that their social performance will not withstand the scrutiny of the people who judge them. As Paul acutely observes, the cultural mould is not to be broken.

Dian, in our next story, finds this out in a rather different way during her employment at a local government personnel office.

Dian's Story: Mr Big's Visit

The first I knew that someone important was in the office was from the fact that the Assistant Personnel Officer was making tea. He had never made his own tea in all the time I had been there. It was accepted that when he wanted tea for himself, or a visitor, somebody else made it for him. But there he was in the kitchen making tea – in a pot and using the posh cups reserved for VIPs. Anyway, an hour or so later, out of his office emerged the Assistant Chief Executive – Mr Big Number 2. The office girls collectively smiled sweetly and tried to look as busy as possible.

This man also happens to be my best friend's father. He is also, fortunately as far as I am concerned, not one to stick to the 'Mr Stuffy' rules adhered to by many of the senior management.

'Yoo hoo', I cried across the office. From there we started our conversation regarding his daughter, and the nasty pair of trousers he had been wearing when I last saw him. We exchanged general fashion insults in a bantering way, while he perched on the edge of my desk. A conversation, I thought. Perfectly natural. I continued my work afterwards as if nothing had happened; to me, nothing of significance had happened.

My boss tended to disagree. Having seen the whole incident I was cross-examined as to why I thought myself able to treat a senior member of staff in such a way, and did I not think it inappropriate for work?

It was not done in a reprimanding manner, more in shock. Even after I had explained the background between myself and the Assistant Chief Executive, the Assistant Personnel Officer still seemed flabbergasted that I did not feel bound by the same culture (of formality to those higher-up the ladder than yourself) that he was. The Assistant Chief Executive seemed very relieved to be able to sit down for a chat as far as I could see, yet my boss was still very disapproving at my behaviour and was unable to accept it for the simple informal chat that it was. As far as I was concerned, it did not upset or disturb any other members of staff, so what was so shocking?

To me, it clearly demonstrated the culture of the organization – the norms of behaviour, perhaps taken to extreme opposites – and the rigidity some people suffered in order to conform to that culture.

I remember thinking at the time how strange my boss was to make such a big thing out of it. I yearned to tell him how stuffy he was being and how stuffy the organization in general could be. However, I simply tried to explain that I did not think it so peculiar to talk to a friend in that manner. The Assistant Chief Executive's reputation for being a little 'alternative' in his approach was well known. He continually shocked people as he waltzed into their office, instead of demanding that they visit him; another unwritten rule.

At the time of the incident I did not take much notice of it. I did not analyse it, or my feelings, as I had no intention of changing my attitude towards senior management. I was polite, yet friendly, worked hard and had respect for those more senior than myself. Why should I change? Looking back, perhaps I was not there long enough to have their culture instilled in me. Perhaps it would have been eventually, but I doubt it. As far as I could see, neither I nor they had anything to gain from me totally conforming to their culture.

I had noticed that most people felt uncomfortable in the presence of my boss, and I heard from many people how they thought that he lacked interpersonal skills. I also found out that, over recent years, he had failed numerous promotion interviews at the shortlist stage. At the time of the incident I decided that perhaps his inability to deviate from his known culture, and accept harmless situations, was one of his downfalls. Unfortunately, at the time, the incident did cause me to lose some respect for my boss; such a small thing should cause him so much anguish.

Whereas Paul was attuned to, and compliant with, the social-performance expectations of his company, Dian stood resolutely outside of some them. In doing so she exposed the taken-for-granted quality of particular behaviours which reinforced status levels in the organization, behaviours which perhaps were no longer necessary. So concerned was the Assistant Personnel Officer to maintain what he regarded as proper decorum in the eyes of his superior that he (a) took personal charge of the tea making and (b) was aghast at the unexpected challenge to usual deference by Dian's casual, familiar approach with his boss. No amount of explanation seemed to satisfy him.

Cultural conditioning can help keep an organization on a particular track. People know where they are in the pecking order; Dian's behaviour threatened this. It can also leave people perpetuating outdated assumptions about how they ought to conduct themselves in a superior/subordinate situation. Understandably, a change in the unwritten rules of personal conduct can be very threatening to someone who, for a long time, has believed that clear signs of deference are important in the presence of a superior. Indeed, even the other office staff were taking no chances with their contrived smiles and business as the boss came into the room. Dian's audacity and independent-mindedness confused the role boundaries which most bureaucratic organizations prefer to maintain – to help people know their place.

For Dian, a temporary member of the organization, the formalities of self-presentation looked absurd. And indeed, like the tale of the emperor's new clothes, we do often delude ourselves that what we are doing in organizations is important and of substance, and we do not want to hear messages to the contrary. If one feels generally insecure in one's role, as the Assistant Personnel Officer seems to have been, there is tendency to play safe and not rock the boat. Dian's *naïveté* in 'yoo-hooing', which happened to be quite acceptable to the Assistant Chief Executive, nevertheless came across as the 'wrong role' in the eyes of her superior (like Minton's performance in the previous story). How can an organization proceed if people simply choose to play whatever part they fancy? And how, the Assistant Personnel Officer might have thought, would Dian's behaviour reflect on him and his career? 'It's alright for her – she's leaving'. But her carefree, uninhibited performance is seen by him as potentially disruptive – what if all other staff decided to emulate her performance?

If we place an individual's performance under a more powerful microscope, its subtleties are fascinating. The following account from Nigel, which merits a close reading, takes us into this detail.

Nigel's Story: Busy, Busy

The following conversation took place one day when the office was short-staffed. The Senior Salesperson of our Engineering Division, Helen, was absent with influenza. Opposite me was her team partner, Jean. Today, as for the past two days, she would be performing Helen's job as well as carrying out any important task relating to her job. I had to answer Helen's phone calls as efficiently as I could and also deal with any work delegated to me by Jean. Helen's workload was accumulating, as was Jean's, whose patience was by now wearing thin as she was feeling the stress and strain of doing two jobs.

Jean: *'Oh I hope Helen's in tomorrow, I couldn't stand another day like yesterday. The 'phones never stopped ringing so I didn't get a chance to shift any of this paperwork. This pile on my desk just keeps growing and growing. I'm going to need a bigger desk soon . . . either that or a bigger waste-bin. I mean, I can't find anything in this mess . . .' (telephone rings).*
'Hello, Product Control here. Oh, hello Bill, how are you today?' (Jean pulls a face and rolls her eyes to the ceiling) . . . 'Alright then Bill, I'll sort it out. Bye!' (she sighs).
'Bloody Bill Dawson. I had enough of him yesterday. He's on the 'phone every ten minutes with the simplest of problems, wasting my time. I'm sure he thinks that all I've got to do all day is answer his calls. Sometimes I just feel like telling him to [telephone rings] tut!' . . .
'Hello, Product Control . . .'
'Oh, that was Alan [her manager]. I've got to pop in and see him. Won't be long.'

She returns about 20 minutes later, red-faced with several more wrinkles on her forehead.

Jean: '*Alan wants me to calculate Steelright's allocation figures for next month. It should have been done yesterday. Honestly, it's one thing after another in this place. I don't know anything about this. Helen usually does it. The problem is Alan wants it done as soon as possible and then he wants their orders entered onto the computer . . . Did anything urgent come up while I was out?*'

Me: '*Well, David Barry rang twice.*'

Jean: '*Yeah, he always says it's urgent but 99 per cent of the time it never is . . . I'll have to call him back later, as it is, I don't think I'm going to meet this deadline. If only I knew how Helen worked out these figures. She keeps meaning to show me but we never seem to have the time. Alan's no help; he's still trying to cope after his promotion from South Yorkshire. It's typical of this place; they promote managers from other Divisions and throw them in the deep end with as little training as possible, so they end up totally confused leaving us to pick up the pieces. Alan's doing his best in the circumstances but Helen and I are practically doing his job for him. Our last manager had a degree in skiving. He left us to sort out his mistakes but they still gave him a promotion. . . . Right, when you've finished that could you enter these Steelright orders onto the system for me? I've managed to work out the figures.*'

Me: '*Yes, no problem.*'

Jean: '*Oh thanks. I don't know what we're going to do when you leave. We really need at least another permanent sales assistant. We keep asking Phil [office manager] for more staff but he hasn't done anything about it since we first approached him three months ago. If you ask me, he's too busy wrapped up in his career and next promotion to be concerned with our problems. One of the problems with this department is that there are more managers than staff. . . . Oh, I'm sorry to keep moaning, but I've had enough for one week.*'

Me: '*Yeah, I know you're usually laughing and telling us all the latest gossip.*'

Jean: '*Hey, that reminds me. I found out some juicy information about Alan. Apparently, when he was in South Yorkshire . . .*' ('phone rings). . . .

> 'Hello, Product Control. Hello David, I was just about to ring you back. . . '

The majority of Jean's comments were not only true of the department, but of the whole Division. Practically everyone you met complained about the large amount of needless paperwork created by the system. Piles of unfinished work lay scattered around the office, meaning that sometimes vital information went missing. Customers were always complaining.

This brief, colourful, clip from office life is probably recognizable to anyone who has spent some time sharing an office. The tittle tattle, we would argue, is full of presentational meanings.

At the broadest level Jean, while undoubtedly highly loaded with work and fraught, wanted to *show* Nigel that not only was she a much put-upon woman (sighs, displays of weariness), but that she had still got the measure of the organization and was in control. So she rolls her eyes when Bill calls, and firmly cuts him down to size *after* he rings off. In this way she uses Nigel as the audience for her display of frustration, something which could not be done directly to Bill. The office arena is a set where the wider dramas of work life can be rehearsed and played out – in safety. Alan, the boss, gets more charitable treatment. Jean shows her deference by dropping her work immediately to attend to his request and later comparing him favourably to the previous 'skiver' manager. Her displeasure with Alan's request for more work is kept at the non-verbal level – the red face and wrinkled forehead.

David Barry, however, is her *bête noire*, the villain of the piece. She 'performs' her dislike of him for Nigel – showing her own power in not returning his call and rubbishing his claims of urgency. However, she cannot jeopardize her actual working relationship with him face to face, or off the office stage. Barry receives the impression that she has been 'just about to phone him back'.

In all this Nigel, the student, is the compliant, safe, catalyst – occasionally helping things along with the odd word or two. Like many office settings, even the relatively silent members are a crucial audience for another's performance. Many offices are real-life soap operas where people build their own set and drama to enact their work and personal frustrations, joys, power and powerlessness. At 5.30 p.m. the office door is locked and the curtain falls.

Thinking On

1 Look back at a recent or ongoing office-type situation. What do you now think was really going on? What do the performances tell you?
2 Can you identify a 'really embarrassing' public moment in your life? What exactly made it embarrassing? What were the consequences?
3 What kinds of job separate public face from private feeling? What are the benefits and costs of this?
4 Do you think that Dian was naïve to behave the way she did in front of Mr Big? Can you imagine what is likely to happen at a subsequent visit?
5 Try to identify the different audiences for Jean's performance, as described by Nigel. In what ways do these audiences differ in their appreciation of the performances?

Reading On

Many of the writings of sociologist Erving Goffman are devoted to understanding the drama and performances of social life, especially his *Presentation of Self in Everyday Life*. This work touches on fascinating details of the performances, and 'props' used by people such as fashion models, clergymen, dentists and beauticians. A summary overview of Goffman's extensive work can be found in Fontana (1980). Performance-principles have been developed in the 'impression management' literature (e.g. Giacalone and Rosenfeld 1991) – how we cultivate particular social appearances. More substantially, the stage and theatre as metaphors for organizational life have been explored by Mangham (1986), Mangham and Overington (1987) and more recently by Hopfl (1995). These authors discuss the 'scripts' we learn to bring about particular role performances, the 'back stage' rehearsals, the 'masks' we don in various circumstances, and what happens when a role performance fails, or 'corpses'. Such analyses suggest that there are dramatic skills associated with all organizational performances, and these skills can be learned.

Are there personal costs to acting out our role performances? The emotional tensions, or 'emotional labour', inherent in the feigning of some performances are well described in a compelling case study of flight attendants by Hochschild (1983) and more comprehensively by Fineman (1993, 1995). Particularly interesting are occupations where a person's performance and 'smile' are very closely scripted by the organization, such as in direct sales jobs, McDonald's and Disneyworld. Van Maanen and Kunda (1991) and Leidner (1991) describe the effects of such work on self-identity. It is worth stressing that the ways *talk* and *language* are used are crucial in shaping performances and impression-making. The content and nuance of talk are part of the business of persuasion. The writings of Mintzberg (1973) and Billig (1987) are of relevance here.

Billig, M. (1987). *Arguing and Thinking: A Rhetorical Approach to Social Psychology*. Cambridge: Cambridge University Press.

Fineman, S. (ed.) (1993). *Emotion in Organizations*. London: Sage.

Fineman, S. (1996). 'Emotion and organizing', in S. Clegg, C. Hardy and W. Nord (eds), *Handbook of Organization Studies*. London: Sage.

Fontana, A. (1980). 'The mask and beyond: the enigmatic sociology of Erving Goffman', in J. Douglas (ed.), *The Sociologies of Everyday Life*. Boston, MA: Allyn and Bacon.

Giacalone, R.A. and Rosenfeld, P.R. (1991). *Applied Impression Management*. Newbury Park, CA: Sage.

Goffman, E. (1959). *The Presentation of Self in Everyday Life*. Garden City, NJ: Anchor Books.

Hochschild, A. (1983). *The Managed Heart*. Berkeley, CA: University of California.

Hopfl, H. (1995). 'Performance and customer service: the cultivation of contempt', *Studies in Cultures, Organizations and Societies*, 1, 47–62.

Leidner, R. (1991). 'Serving hamburgers and selling insurance: gender, work and identity in interactive service jobs', *Gender and Society*, 5, 2, 154–77.

Mangham, I.L. (1986). *Power and Performance in Organizations*. Oxford: Blackwell.

Mangham, I.L. and Overington, M.A. (1987). *Organizations as Theatre*. Chichester: Wiley.

Mintzberg, H. (1973). *The Nature of Managerial Work*. New York: Harper and Row.

Van Maanen, J. (1991). 'The smile factory: work at Disneyland', in P.J. Frost, L.F. Moore, M.R. Pierre, C.C. Lundberg and J. Martin (eds), *Reframing Organizational Culture*. Newbury Park, CA: Sage.

Van Maanen, J. and Kunda, G. (1989). '"Real feelings": emotional expression and organizational culture', *Research in Organizational Behavior*, 11, 43–103.

3

Red Tape

When thinking about large organizations, few ideas and images come to mind as readily as 'bureaucracy'. Whatever sociology books tell us about bureaucracy, its meaning includes qualities like rigidity, aversion to responsibility, slowness, inefficiency. No single term captures these negative qualities as aptly as 'red tape'. Numerous stories supplied by students focus on this theme, which lends itself to endless variations – cock-ups, absurdities, delays and petty-mindedness. The emotions evoked by red tape include bewilderment and confusion, fatalism and defiance, amusement and despair, but above all *frustration*.

Nearly all stories which focus on red tape pitch the individual as a creative person, with initiative, imagination and common sense against the blind and impersonal forces of bureaucracy. The outcomes of this confrontation vary. Who wins? Does the individual standing up to bureaucracy triumph, or does he or she give up and become a part of the impersonal forces? Does the individual lose his or her ability to criticize the organization, or can he or she still see the funny side and laugh at it?

In the first story, Anders, a Swedish student, describes some of the difficulties in getting a relatively simple job done in an insurance company.

Anders's Story: Winning Teams? You Must be Kidding!

I woke up to the tunes of Jazz FM; another day in the bureaucracy I thought. Took a shower, got dressed, breakfast in front of the TV, the usual routine. I had been with the company for about three months and I enjoyed it most of the time – but with a few reservations.

I arrived at the office and began my usual tasks when the phone rang. It was a lady from a business unit whose finance we handled. She explained that one of her staff had had an accident and could not attend a 'Building Winning Teams' course due to start the following Monday.

I took down the details of the matter and went over to my manager. I explained the situation and we both agreed that we should explore the possibilities of sending someone else to attend the course or get a refund. I offered to follow it up and my manager approved.

My first action was to contact the lady who had called me to ask her about the costs of the course; £750 she said. So I asked whether we would get our money back or not. This she hadn't looked into nor was she planning to do, she explained. I realized that she was not too concerned. If anyone was going to resolve the problem, I had to deal with it myself. So, I got in touch with the Personnel Department to ask whether we could get any money back or not.

They asked if it was an external or an internal course, and I explained what kind of course it was. They informed me that it was a mix of both and that they didn't know if it was possible to get a refund. So I had to ask how I could find this out. 'Try the course coordinator', was the answer. I called him but he was busy on another line and his assistant couldn't answer my question. So I asked for him to call me when he was free. After one hour's wait I tried again and got through. I was informed that there was no possibility of a refund but that we could send someone else if we wished.

So I went to work on that. I began by asking the department where the injured person worked, but they expressed no further interest. So I turned elsewhere. Eventually, after many more phone calls, I found someone who wanted to, was allowed, and eventually did, attend the course.

When I look back at this incident, the most significant thing now seems to be the extent to which my behaviour was 'shaped' by the organization. Instead of directly questioning whether we could send someone else or get a refund, I simply passed on the message to my manager for further instructions. This is what the hierarchy expected from me and this is what I did – without any trace of personal initiative. I am now surprised by the fact that I found myself working in a way which was very unlike me and very irrational. I felt like I had left parts of my brain at home.

I believe that a lot of other people in the company functioned in the same manner. None of the people involved in the incident put in any extra effort to try to solve the problem. The lady at the start of the story didn't bother to inform the course coordinator about her subordinate's accident, nor did she explore any possibilities of sending someone else or getting a refund. She just looked for someone to pass the buck to, which, as it turned out, was also my first instinct – to pass it on to someone else. Nor did the staff in Personnel try to help. There was a general lack of concern for the company's well-being. Money is no matter – as long as it's not my own – seemed to be the general motto. In spite of living with a constant threat of redundancies, no one seemed to mind about the company's money being wasted. I found this quite strange.

On a personal level this was probably the best day of my placement. I experienced many different things and was able to develop my interpersonal skills further. More importantly, I managed to overcome my instinct of passing the buck, like everyone else, and get it sorted out by myself. At the end of the day, I felt that I had achieved something. Through the day I was motivated by many different things. At first I was hoping that I might attend the course myself, but as time passed it was the satisfaction and appreciation I felt that really mattered. If others had a chance to experience such feelings, their attitudes towards their colleagues, the company, and work in general, would change – and it could make a great difference for the company.

In resolving what seems like a small problem caused by an accident, Anders comes face to face with numerous features of red tape: passing the buck, never finding the 'right' person, constantly meeting people too busy on other things, wasting of time and resources, as well as a complete lack of teamwork. It is the story's supreme irony (not commented upon by Anders) that the whole thing revolves around a place on a course called 'Building a Winning Team'.

Anders was surprised by several things. He was astonished by the indifference of employees towards the waste of company money, and the ease with which they disowned problems; but he was also concerned by the extent to which he had adopted his organization's bad habits – to the point where they became 'instinctive', with his brain switching on to autopilot. Yet, what made the incident memorable was that it finally forced him to snap out of this mode of operation, to cut through the red tape by sheer perseverance. The incident reasserted his own personal qualities over the stultifying effects of the organization and marked a small triumph of the human factor against bureaucratic inertia.

Anders is perhaps a little artless in thinking that if only other members of organizations had similar experiences they might undergo a collective change of attitudes and mentality. His own account, as well as the images of organizations evoked by the stories which follow in this chapter, show how difficult this is.

Yet, the story has another facet. It reveals that, even in profoundly bureaucratic organizations, we meet people willing to put enormous efforts into sorting out a difficulty, serving a customer, or helping a colleague in trouble. Would it not have been easier for Anders to give up after the umpteenth unsuccessful telephone call and conclude that there was nothing to be done? A less persistent person might have done just this, hoping that his own, otherwise preoccupied, manager would forget about this small issue. The odds that he would get into serious trouble for failing to sort it out would be minimal. But, with every reversal, Anders got more hooked into the case, determined to see it through. This is sometimes referred to as 'escalation of commitment', and can lead to a sense of triumph when one's efforts are finally rewarded with success. Alternatively, it can lead to great disasters, especially if a person becomes obsessed with an unattainable objective.

Significantly, Anders never appears to ask himself if his great efforts were, after all, expended on a worthwhile cause. To be sure, he managed to get someone to attend the £750 course, though this by itself may seem scant reward. A company that seems generally to care little for individual development will benefit only very modestly from sending isolated employees on courses for 'Building Winning Teams'. The failure to question the ultimate aim of one's efforts, and becoming preoccupied with the getting 'the job' done, is a classic trait of bureaucracy: the domination of means over goals, of 'how to' over 'why'.

Anders's story highlights the ability of individuals to prevail over bureaucratic red tape. The second story in this chapter, told by Jan, reveals how easily they can get their fingers burnt when using their initiative – in what they see as the organization's interest.

Jan's Story: The Watchdogs

My main job was to make a database of swaps, sales and purchases of Brazilian debt, undertaken by the bank since 1988. The data were filed at many different locations in the City, so I suggested to my manager that I should use my private portable PC to enter the data in each location. My manager thought it was a great idea.

Three months into my placement I was using a new software program when the screen suddenly turned black with lots of star-shaped objects flicking on and off all over the monitor. I thought it might be a virus, and immediately showed it to my manager. He suggested calling the bank's internal computer unit to fix it. When he called them, the response was immediate. A woman from the unit called me within half a minute, and started asking me questions:

'Are you the person who uses a private PC to do bank work?'
'Yes.'
'And you have a virus on your machine?'
'I'm not sure, but I suspect I have.'
'For how long have you used your machine doing bank work?'
'Three months.'
'Have you read the bank's internal software rules and regulations?'
'No.'
'Have you used your disks on any of the Bank's computers?'
'Just to copy files onto disks.'
'Did you know it is a criminal offence to use unauthorized software on the bank's machines?'
'No.'
'Switch off your computer! We'll come right over!'

Five minutes later three people burst into the office. The voice from the phone continued to fire questions at me. She wrote down everything I said. The other two started to feed virus-detection programs into my machine. They became notably anxious as I showed them the working station I had used for disk copying. That machine was linked to the Bank's national computer link in Bradford!

After they had scanned my PC, it turned out to be perfectly clean. What I thought to be a virus turned out to be nothing but the 'save screen' facility of the software. I was not allowed to use my PC on the Bank's premises again.

This episode made me look differently at the organization I was working for. Before the incident I really did not feel restricted in any way by rules or regulations. It seemed like everything was OK, as long as you did your job. But as I found out, it did not take much for the watchdogs of the organization to come racing out of their hide-outs to protect it, destroying my early perception of the bank as an 'easy going' establishment.

Subsequently, the Computer Unit had a meeting with my manager who came over to talk to me about what they had discussed. It seems that the bank's regulations regarding use of private PCs at work were not precise in their existing form. The computer unit told us that they would take this incident to the very top to ban bank work on private machines. I never saw any circular actually setting out a ban. I can only speculate, but such a proposal probably met considerable resistance from the top management. They know that many managers at varying levels, do take work home on disks. Such a ban would also be impossible to enforce.

After this incident, my progress on the database was considerably slowed down. I spent a lot of time actually collecting information at different locations before going back to the office to input the data. I suggested to my manager that I could continue to use my computer at home to catch up with some work (I used to work a bit at home during weekends), but he said no. It wasn't worth taking any more chances.

The whole episode seemed very unfair to me at the time. I had showed initiative in bringing in my own PC to save time. The bank's way of showing gratitude was to cross-examine me at the first sign of possible trouble. Later I heard that the reason for taking down all those details was for use in a possible lawsuit against me, in case I had infected the national computer link with a virus.

When I look back at what happened, I can now fully understand the computer engineers' concern. Since my return to the university, I have seen one virus wreak havoc at the computer lab of the School of Management, and all it takes is copying a single disk! I have now installed a virus protection program on my computer!

I reckon that showing initiative is not always positive in large organizations – it can backfire if something goes wrong.

Jan's experience brought him face to face with a darker side of his organization, one which was not evident behind the friendly and relaxed front. In his story he saw himself as someone pursued by pitiless watchdogs and confronted with Draconian penalties for showing initiative. The fact that he had asked his manager's permission before using his machine is never brought up as an excuse, nor is the fact that his manager failed to cover him. Yet, what gives the story a slightly Kafkaesque quality is that, at the end of Jan's intimidating ordeal, it turns out that the bank did *not* have regulations explicitly banning the use of private computers:

Jan's 'criminal offence' only existed in the mind of the 'voice from the phone'.

What does the incident reveal about bureaucratic regulations? Clearly, Jan appears to end his account by deferring to their rationality, in spite of the inconvenience and inefficiency which they cause. His manager confirms the view that it is not worth taking risks, and he seems to surrender his initiative. The incident upset him sufficiently for him to resist disregarding or bending bureaucratic procedures in future. This may be the 'wrong' lesson to carry from such an incident, but it aptly demonstrates how easily a person's resourcefulness can be choked by potential victimization and fear. What can result is a defensive attitude, summed up by 'cover your back'.

The next story also shows how easily innovativeness, questioning and originality can be thwarted by organizational rules. Yet it indicates that, even in highly bureaucratic organizations, rules can and are routinely broken. It was reported by Alexander, who worked for a major department store in the centre of London. Again, computers are the focus of concern.

Alexander's Story: Can't be Done!

During my placement I was asked to complete a project. My report had to be presented to one of the principal directors, the Head of Graduate Recruitment, and to some other senior managers within the store. The presentation was to be in the form of a discussion based on a written report. I had no access to a word processor, so I presumed I would be using one of the PCs in the store.

I made an appointment to see the Staff Trainer during which I asked her about the possibility of using the PC – either at lunchtime or after the store had closed. I was told that Security locked up the store twenty minutes after closing, and so evening use was not feasible. She also said that, due to employment law, I was not allowed to work through my lunch break.

The store wasn't open on Mondays, so I enquired about using one then, offering to do unpaid overtime work. This would not be possible either, said the Staff Trainer. The company didn't like people working on their day off.

Frustrated, I returned to my department and related the story to my Department Manager. She was furious, and phoned the Managing Director of the store to complain. I was immediately given full access to the computers on Mondays, and was even offered a couple of short sessions on how to use them.

The difficulty was resolved and the presentation went very well, but I was able to understand a lot about the company from this affair. Attitudes of individuals towards rules and regulations are dependent on their age and length of service with the company. My Departmental Manager was fairly young and hadn't been with the company for very long; she was flexible with the rules. She treated the rules as an aid to running the business but also saw the need to adapt or even break them from time to time – for the good of the business. The Managing Director was also fairly new to the company and his decision was based on logical reasoning. He was not blinkered by the overbearing power of rules. The Staff Trainer, on the other hand, had been in the company for a considerable time. She had become part of the rules herself; she was as rigid as they were. She was unable to see past the letter of the regulations. It seemed easy for her to say 'no' to everything running against the rules, but I think that it went even deeper than this. She really believed this was always the way to do things.

Sticking to the rules was not only a management phenomenon, it could be seen at every level of the hierarchy. Those who had been in the store for a long time were mocked by the newer recruits as the 'family'. They were also known as 'purples' after the company's logo and the colour of its lorries. This 'purple' image also stemmed from the fact that only the company chairman was allowed to write in purple ink!

I must also admit that I saw a change in myself over the six-month placement. At first, I was quick to question the company's way of tackling certain aspects of its business (e.g. merchandising and display techniques), but I gradually lost my motivation when the only answer I received was 'that's the way we like it done'. It became less hassle just to accept the way it was done than to create ill feeling by questioning it. In sum, I think that it was too easy for everyone just to accept the rules as they stood without really thinking about the consequences of them.

Like Jan's story, Alexander's ends up in disillusionment and fatalism – though not before he, with the help of his immediate manager, and no less a figure than the Managing Director, succeeded in overcoming one of the obstacles barring his path. Moreover, Alexander does not pretend that red tape is a corruption of what was originally a rational set of rules. Instead, he views it as a feature of a company which badly needs a breath of fresh air, a legacy of a stale tradition and culture. Not only rules and regulations, but other practices and conventions are accepted unquestioningly – at least by the majority, for whom they become second nature. It is not fear, but the hassle of questioning what others have absorbed that eventually drives him to conform to the company's stuffy traditionalism.

Yet, Alexander's story shows that organizational rules can be bent and a blind eye turned. The Managing Director, in effect, redefined the rule which says 'No work on Mondays' to mean 'No work on Mondays, unless absolutely necessary, unless the employee is willing to work on Mondays, and unless he or she does not demand extra money for it.' But this redefinition does not necessarily mean an actual change in rules. Trying to change the 'No work on Mondays' rule is likely to incite a hostile response from older staff, so the original rule may stay in the 'book', but simply become less-stringently applied – a slight bending.

The final story, recounted by Geir, eloquently contrasts the failure to observe fire regulations, in a financial securities corporation, with the extreme formality governing other aspects of office conduct.

Geir's Story: 'Rules are Rules! Sometimes.'

A fire alarm sounded loudly from the corridor outside, and everyone in the office looked up irritably. The announced fire exercise was meant to test the emergency preparedness of the company. Outside, the rain was driven against the windows by the force of the wind and the temperature was scarcely above freezing.

The formal procedure upon the sound of the alarm is to evacuate the building. All unnecessary items are to be left behind, and the work with which one is occupied is to be abandoned. We are then to collect at certain designated areas. However, formal procedures didn't appear to be at the top of the agenda in the office this day. Most people just continued their work, the rhythmic bursts of ringing from the alarm an accompaniment for the tapping of keyboards and the sound of telephone conversations.

The manager was one of two fire marshals for the whole floor. He was sitting by his desk working, ignoring the cacophony. The marshal's armband he had been displaying earlier with such pride was tucked away in a drawer. Contrary to his instructions, he actually suggested people should ignore the alarm in order to deal with the pressing nature of the work. This sentiment was largely echoed by the supervisors. Those few of us who, after completing our immediate tasks, felt ready to brave the cold and the rain, actually felt a bit guilty for 'using' the opportunity to leave work for a while.

The episode was not unique. Earlier, there had been false alarms which had been totally ignored, people working straight through them. When someone raised the question of acting on the alarm, the manager took it as a joke. Yet, neither jokes nor the lax attitude shown towards emergency procedures and other organizational formalities (security checks, locking of documents, use of passwords, etc.) were shown towards the formalities of other office routines. The opposite was the case here.

No messing about was tolerated in the office. A couple of times, I tried to read an article in the paper whilst in the office, but this was not allowed; I was told to get on with my work. The same happened when people tried to keep up with the latest news on Thatcher's resignation or the start of the Gulf War. On a couple of occasions, I tried to introduce a degree of friendliness into letters I was about to send to clients, and I made the mistake of letting a supervisor see them. Not even a little 'Merry Christmas' at the bottom of the letter was acceptable.

To sum up, I would say that some of the wider, organizational formalities were not taken very seriously. The manager and some of the supervisors encouraged us to ignore them – if they impeded the activity of the office. Yet, the same characters enforced specific office formalities, allowing no laxity at all.

Geir's account draws a sharp distinction between those bureaucratic rules which are openly dismissed as a joke and those that are strictly enforced. What is especially noteworthy is that, whether a rule is observed or not has little to do with its rationality or expediency. The risk of a fire, most people would agree, is rather more serious than the risk of offending a client by including 'Merry Christmas' at the end of a letter. Yet, in many organizations management appears to be more concerned about tiny variations from established practice, which are seen as the thin-end of a wedge leading to chaos: 'Merry Christmas today, pink paper tomorrow and the end of civilization the day after'.

Deviating in small ways from normal rules is one way of individualizing work, and giving it new meaning. But such touches can, all too easily, be misread as signs of defiance or a collapse of discipline. They can be stamped upon fairly easily. Deeper threats, on the other hand, are less visible, their effects far less direct and harder to control. For some companies, especially those facing substantial organizational difficulties, it is easier to focus on the minutiae of discipline and control, than on the more major problems of, say, innovation, morale, markets and products.

The stories in this chapter highlight the considerable constraints that organizations place on our students' freshness, initiative and individuality, and the fatalism with which the students accepted and internalized the restrictions. Yet, they also show how individuals can, and do, take on bureaucratic procedure, in order to do their job better.

The stories also reveal the ambivalence that bureaucratic routines and regulations can generate. On the one hand, we experience acute frustration, especially when they stand in the way of us achieving our short-term goals. On the other hand, we find that we need them to guide and protect us. As all four of our students discovered, there is something highly reassuring and comforting about sticking-to-the-rules without questioning them; and yet, at the same time, they all feel uncomfortable about being reduced to one-dimensional organizational men (like the ones they encountered in their textbooks).

Not for nothing have rules and regulations been described as the opium of bureaucratic officials. Without rules, they feel exposed, paralysed and even lost; with them, they are people of authority. Interestingly, the entire rhetoric of recent management theory and practice has come to hinge on the dismantling of bureaucracy, the tearing down of pyramids and the undermining of rules and regulations. Yet clearly, as demonstrated by our students, the rule-bound organization is far from dead, and the informal organizational processes which redefine these rules are still highly active.

Thinking On

1 Does bureaucratic red tape serve *any* useful purpose? If so, what?

2 Is it true that bending the rules leads to ever-increasing violations, ending up in complete anarchy? Think of some examples where you witnessed rules being bent or broken, and assess their consequences.

3 Popular shows and serials frequently satirize bureaucracy and joke at its absurdities. For example, a nurse is shown

waking up a patient in order to give him his sleeping pill. Can you think of some jokes based on dumb bureaucrats? What makes such jokes funny?

4 Rules are rules, and yet rules do not have the same meaning for everybody. Reflect on a set of rules which turned out to have very different meanings to different individuals.

5 Why do you think that Anders was landed with the problem he was? How might you have responded if you had received a similar telephone call to the one he did? What would then have happened to 'the problem'?

6 Can you envisage a set of rules which would have averted Jan's unpleasant experience in using his own computer at work? Do you think that he was right in showing the initiative that he did?

7 Is there significance in the fact that computers feature centrally in two of the four stories of this chapter? What difficulties does the use of computers generate for organizations?

8 In what circumstances do rules, regulations and procedures in organizations actually change? What pressures bring about such changes?

Reading On

Bureaucracy is one of the most popular subjects in the study of organizations. Many theorists have engaged with Weber's theory of bureaucracy which envisaged an ideal type of bureaucracy as the most efficient form of administration. Gouldner (1954), for example, sought to distinguish between rational rules, punitive rules and mock rules (like the fire regulations in Geir's story), whereas theorists like Jaques (1976) and Drucker (1989) have elaborated and refined arguments of how organizational efficiency can be enhanced through planning, procedures, rules and control.

Peters and Waterman (1982) and numerous other writers, on the other hand, have attacked bureaucracy as the cause of virtually every organizational ill and have advocated more loosely-structured organizations, coupled with strong organizational values and a heavy reliance on individual initiative as the recipe for success. Numerous writings by successful businessmen have attacked bureaucracy along similar lines, notably Carlzon (1989), Morita (1987) and Roddick (1991). Charles Handy (1976) has argued that bureaucracy is itself a feature of the culture of certain organizations, which he terms 'role cultures', whereas other cultures (including power cultures, task cultures and support cultures) lay far less emphasis on standardized procedures and regulations. The psychological dependence of individuals on procedures and rules is graphically depicted by Sims et al. (1993).

The material presented in this chapter also addresses issues of power and control in organizations. Rules in organizations, like the laws of wider society, are not merely means for the achievement of agreed-upon goals, they are also mechanisms of control, safeguarding the interests of those in positions of power. Robert Michels (1949), arguing against Weber's view of rational bureaucracy, envisaged bureaucracy as a smokescreen behind which a ruthless power game goes on, a game through which the few rule the many. This is what he described as the 'Iron Law of Oligarchy'. Two chapters in Morgan's (1986) *Images of Organization* discuss organizations as political systems and as instruments of domination – both are of considerable use to the reader who wishes to explore further the political dimension of the stories introduced in this chapter.

In a series of pioneering studies focusing on the mental asylum, the prison, the clinic, the army and the school, Michel Foucault (1965, 1971, 1976, 1977) has argued that these institutions signal the arrival of a new type of control over the masses, a form of control pervasive enough to be absorbed into each and every individual's subjectivity. Rules and bureaucratic procedures of observation, classification and punishment are, according to this view, powerful instruments of control not because of their tangible, visible effects, but because they create a pliant, self-controlled, disciplined population who are unable to envisage themselves outside of these procedures. Our society becomes saturated with ever-vigilant watchdogs, like the ones pursuing Jan.

A number of neo-Marxist theorists have developed theories of resistance, sometimes drawing on Foucault's work, according to which organizational subordinates can find more or less indirect ways of contesting, undermining or evading control mechanisms, such as those embodied in rules and regulations. (See Knights and Willmott 1990; Jermier et al. 1994.) According to these arguments, there are instances when organizational red tape (such as that encountered in this chapter) is neither a dysfunction of bureaucracy nor a smoke-screen for management control but rather an attempt by subordinates to reclaim some control through excessive or ritualistic adherence to rules and procedures.

The stories in this chapter also raise two further issues. Readers interested in the concept of escalation of commitment should consult Staw and Ross (1987) and Ross and Staw (1993). Readers interested in the theme of computers at the workplace and the way they affect power and control are directed to Buchanan and Boddy (1983), Forester (1989), Gabriel (1992), O'Connell Davidson (1994) and Chapter 8 of Sims et al. (1993).

Buchanan, D.A. and Boddy, D. (1983). *Organizations in the Computer Age*. Aldershot: Gower.

Carlzon, J. (1989). *Moments of Truth*. New York: Harper and Row.

Drucker, P.F. (1989). *The Practice of Management*. Oxford: Heinemann.

Forester, T. (ed.) (1989). *Computers in the Human Context: Information Technology, Productivity and People*. Oxford: Basil Blackwell.

Foucault, Michel (1965). *Madness and Civilization*. New York: Random House.

Foucault, Michel (1971). *The Birth of the Clinic*. London: Tavistock.

Foucault, Michel (1976). *The History of Sexuality*. Harmondsworth: Penguin.

Foucault, Michel (1977). *Discipline and Punish*. London: Allen and Unwin.

Gabriel, Yiannis (1992). 'Heroes, villains, fools and magic wands: computers in organizational folklore', *International Journal of Information Resource Management*, 3, 1, 3–12.

Gouldner, A.W. (1954). *Patterns of Industrial Bureaucracy*. Glencoe, IL: Free Press.

Handy, C.B. (1976). *Understanding Organizations*. Harmondsworth: Penguin.

Jaques, E. (1976). *A General Theory of Bureaucracy*. Oxford: Heinemann.

Jermier, J.M., Knights, D. and Nord, W.R. (eds) (1994). *Resistance and Power in Organizations*. London: Routledge.

Knights, D. and Willmott, H. (eds) (1990). *Labour Process Theory*. Basingstoke: Macmillan.

Michels, R. (1949). *Political Parties*. New York: Free Press.

Morgan, Gareth (1986). *Images of Organization*. Beverly Hills, CA: Sage.

Morita, A. (1987). *Made in Japan*. London: Fontana.

O'Connell Davidson, Julia (1994). 'The sources and limits of resistance in a privatized utility', in J.M. Jermier, D. Knights and W.R. Nord (eds), *Resistance and Power in Organizations*. London: Routledge.

Peters, T. and Waterman, R.H. (1982). *In Search of Excellence*. New York: Harper and Row.

Roddick, A. (1991). *Body and Soul*. London: Ebury Press.

Ross, J. and Staw, B.M. (1993). 'Organizational escalation and exit: lessons from the Shoreham Nuclear Power Plant', *Academy of Management Journal*, 36, 701–32.

Sims, D., Fineman, S. and Gabriel, Y. (1993). *Organizing and Organizations: An Introduction*. London: Sage.

Staw, B.M. and Ross, J. (1987). 'Understanding escalations situations: antecedents, prototypes and solutions', in B.M. Staw and L.L. Cummings (eds), *Research in Organizational Behavior*, 9. Greenwich, CT: JAI Press.

4

Functions and Ceremonies

Organizational life is often punctuated by functions and ceremonies. Some are knitted into the formal business of the enterprise – launching a new product, opening a factory or building, introducing new recruits to the organization's style, products and services. Others are tied less to the work in hand, aimed at the expression of feeling or personal acknowledgement – such as reward ceremonies, the annual Christmas party, celebrating a retirement. Certain functions act as rites of passage, marking the process of, for example, joining an organization, getting promoted or leaving. They provide a public acknowledgement, legitimating a significant change in work role or status; people now know your new place.

There are ceremonies which have a long history of obscure origins. Their deep-rootedness has given them a meaning, momentum and integrity; they 'need' to happen simply because they have always happened. Ancient ceremonies associated with parliamentary procedure, royal occasions, military protocol or a school's traditions are of this ilk. However, there is another agenda which interests us – what they reveal, sometimes starkly, about organizational values, politics and relationships.

The 'dressing' or staging of different functions is itself a symbol of image – which may or may not correspond to what organizational members actually believe or do. Also, the very infrequency of certain events offers people an unusual opportunity to behave and interact in ways which free them from the normal constraints of their role – occasionally with embarrassing consequences.

The three stories that follow are told by Andrew, Mark and Bill, each of whom worked for a different, large corporation. Andrew tells of what happened at a major orientation conference on the second day of his employment with a computer organization. Mark worked for an accountancy firm which, with elaborate ceremony, introduced him to its corporate values. The final story is Bill's: a reflection on his parting from a transport services company, his insights drawn from the machinations of a farewell dinner, held in his honour.

Andrew's Story: 'You Must be New!'

At eight-thirty on day two at Computam, I was accompanied into a large room full of around thirty of the conference delegates, to be indoctrinated with 'Customer Care – The Computam Way' for the next ten hours. Having to start a new job with a week's warning in a new and alien environment is daunting enough without the thought of attending an internal conference with the company's entire Logistics Division. The content of the programme is immaterial except to provide an understanding of the image Computam was portraying to its workforce, all of whom were required to attend similar events.

'Honesty', I uttered in reply to an open question on what the public expected from Computam. 'You must be new!', came the reply which was met with universal hilarity. In a different context this would have been meant as a genuine joke, but less than a few minutes later the mood of the conference had changed to one of confrontation between the departmental managers and the two members of the upper management, chairing the conference. The departmental managers were complaining that the ideal of implementing customer care throughout Computam was simply unworkable. Upper management had slashed the budgets and narrowed margins, making implementation of the new time-consuming tasks a low, even non-existent, priority.

'The structure of Computam is too bureaucratic and full of overburdened men', was one quote from my newly acquired manager, 'more than the National Health Service or the Government'.

'Computam's public profile is very limited', stated another unknown face, 'especially when compared with IBM who we are supposed to be competing against.'

'With our department', joined in another, 'there is no organizational map and we have no fixed contacts with the customer to help us implement these objectives.'

By the end of my second day's employment with Computam I had realized that I wasn't employed by quite the smooth running, structurally sound company that I had imagined Computam to be. The public image of Computam was the only contact I had previously experienced with the company – slick presentations and motivating statements, such as 'We are going to be number one global IT company' and 'We will exceed customer expectations – not merely meet them'.

I remember feeling proud to be a member of this international conglomerate that was generating enthusiasm and loyalty amongst all its employees. Or was it? Or was it just me? Maybe the presentation I was seeing was a bit too idealistic to be taken as read. But surely the feeling of common corporate identity was binding us, the Computam employees, together. How naïve a young student trainee can be! On a few occasions, when a few people laughed at certain corporate statements, I thought I'd missed an in-joke. The joke turned out to be centred on Computam itself.

Having your illusions shattered is a thought-provoking experience. And seeing such internal conflict on my second day, working for a company I thought I knew, definitely changed the way I then went on to interact with people within the company. What had I been taught? That the problem with so many large organizations is the bureaucratic red tape that shadows anything anyone attempts to do. As I sat in the conference room, surrounded by portraits of board members, my mind returned to lecture halls and tedious theories of organizational structure. To say that theory had turned into reality may seem to be a gross cliché but I remember feeling how ironic the situation was and how well it fitted into everything I had learnt.

The incident also taught me a lot about the people I would be working with. I had felt very isolated sitting in a room full of strangers who, I felt, along with myself, were all being indoctrinated with 'big brother' philosophies and ideals. Seeing the way many of the members of my department were fighting against the bureaucratic upper management gave me a sense of belonging and security as I realized that I was part of a team and not a machine.

Writing about this incident now, I must admit that I again feel a sense of ironic humour, but for entirely different reasons. Everything I have written seems a nice fitting of theory to reality. If it were not for the lectures I had sat through on bureaucratic organizations, the incident would probably have been a lot more disturbing and worrying to a new employee such as myself. But the incident was a perfect case study for several first-year lectures – a bit too perfect not to generate a smile! I guess the moral of the story is that inside every bureaucratic machine there are always characters fighting against the bureaucracy. Often the external image of a company is quite removed from the internal reality – but you can never know that until you are part of that internal reality.

The organization, or more precisely the top management, in this story, had unwittingly created an arena where long-standing gripes and disaffections could surface. Once debunked, the ceremonial setting exposes its architects to criticism and old grievances.

High profile slogans of 'care' are easily turned against the 'enemy': top management. There is safety in large numbers; individuals feel emboldened and protected by the group. They can take more risks and speak out – directly, or coded in jokes and humour. In normal work relationships the hierarchical effect of position and power is more marked, so it can be far more difficult for a subordinate to challenge a superior. A conference or a function provides at least a partial amnesty, allowing the voicing of criticisms that are normally silenced. After all, managers would be loath to spoil a party they have themselves organized.

The assembled employees do not raise a cheer for the company way – a stalled attempt at cultural engineering. As the student rapidly learns, the company's glossy image is just that. To move beyond this to deeper change, requires considerable trust, and that needs to be built up from the basic working relationships and participation at all levels of the organization. Without this foundation, grand indoctrination events end up reproducing existing social differences in the organization. So our student leaves somewhat stunned, but as a willing new recruit to the 'them-and-us' culture.

Andrew speaks of having his illusions shattered. Organizations trade in illusions at two major levels. The first is public image – broadcast to potential recruits and to customers. Brochures and advertisements are designed by skilled public relations professionals to present a polished and selective image of the organization, one that will attract the reader's attention. 'Truth' is adjusted to a particular purpose or goal – to get a recruit, to win a customer. Some people argue this is unwarranted deception; others point out that few areas of life are free from selective distortions – but we must avoid downright lies.

The second illusion is to maintain, within the organization, a clear, strategic, managerial view of what the organization should be. Mission statements, appeals to the wisdom of founding fathers, logos and training sessions are harnessed for this purpose. Yet, the political realities, or pluralism, of organizational life suggests that even the best of managerial intentions often have to give way to collisions, conflicts and non-managerial interests. Such differences are ignored at management's peril. This much Andrew had begun to learn.

Mark's Story: 'A New Marketing Strategy'

In November, Smithsons presented their new marketing strategy to their employees: ten core values, that we'd live our professional and personal lives by. The launch in the Southampton office was an after-work presentation by the four office partners, with a delectable buffet laid on. They used slides, a video (with U2 soundtrack) and various marketing materials including an A4 presentation card and credit card sized prompter, in case we ever forgot them.

I was fresh faced and back from weeks of training courses. I'd been indoctrinated into the Smithsons' way of doing everything. I sat next to the two most senior audit managers. As the evening progressed, my rapt attention was disturbed by these two managers, who were ridiculing everything that was said. The A4 card would 'look nice on the toilet wall' and the strategy would 'last five minutes'! It was like sitting at the back of a classroom next to the troublemakers and I felt uncomfortable! With hindsight, I would have joined in . . .

The climax of the evening was the announcement that the office had been set a challenge. We'd been split into groups and were to present a report on one core value. The report was to include the strengths and weaknesses of the Southampton office in regard to the core value, and to possible improvements. The prize was a hamper to be presented at the Christmas dinner.

All reports were dutifully handed in, in roughly the same format, except for one group, which adopted a satirical approach. They believed their uniqueness would win. For example, their report in relation to the core value, 'taking a long-term view', contained the following statement: 'Is the best way to get our fee to recommend full-scale redundancy?'

The two managers responsible were called in by the tax partner and given a 'stern telling off'. The incident was hushed up, but due to the lack of scandal in the office, it spread like wildfire.

Smithsons merged with Johnson in the early 1990s. The Johnson Southampton office thought it more of an invasion, as Smithsons' London staff were brought in to fill managerial positions. The Johnson partner-in-charge was demoted. The cultures of the firms clashed. Johnson's were 'hard work but social time is important'. Smithsons emphasized, 'work harder, play less'. The Johnson partner-in-charge had been at the forefront of social events. After the merger he disappeared from the social scene. Possibly having something to prove, he now worked all hours. I noted that the new recruits wholeheartedly accepted Smithsons' practice, but the Johnson's people were more sceptical.

The core values presentation was everything I thought was good about Smithsons – professional and effective. On reflection, I was naïve, though I'm proud of having worked there. Observing the audit managers being blasé about an important (I thought) strategy made me think. They were the representative face of Smithsons in the field, and they'd got where they were now by being professional. But their cynicism made me examine critically what I saw. On examination, the core values might apply equally to any firm that wanted to be 'the best'.

The offending report writers were ex-Johnson staff, subtly showing their dissatisfaction with the way they felt they'd been treated. The blanketing made it impossible to see a copy of the full report and no one in their group would talk about it. I believe the partners did not want such unprofessional behaviour from managers undermining the core values' importance to the other staff.

This led me to question the relationship between the staff and partners. The profit drive is very evident. In audit, everything revolves around recovery (fee/costs) and each minute has to be accounted for. In audit planning, it was ensuring that all risks to the firm (partners) were covered; client service came second. A genuine complaint about lack of communication and socializing between the partners and staff was expressed in the reports: 'Partners should be down the pub on Fridays with ears and wallets open.' 'I knew we'd bought a computer company from reading a local newspaper – two weeks before any official word.'

The whole incident taught me more about the firm, than weeks of courses did. It made me aware of how a culture clash can divide an organization. More importantly, I learnt to question everything, and that a healthy dose of cynicism is essential for life!

In this story, like the previous one, an event meant as a celebration of corporate values generates a lively counter-culture – opposition to top management attempts to control what others in the organization should feel or believe. Most significantly, it reveals the legacy of unhealed wounds – from the recent marrying of two different corporations, notionally in the same business, but very different in cultural background. Often mergers and acquisitions take place for 'sound economic' reasons, but underestimate the problems of assimilating two different traditions. Also present in this account is the deep irony, soon spotted by Mark's innocent eye, that the dominant value in the company's actual practice – financially accounting for every last detail of work done – is the very one omitted from the rather nobler list of company values.

Resistance to the company's dominant, that is top management, culture is risky. On the one hand Mark is a reasonably safe, wide-eyed, new recruit to the 'toilet wall' club of the senior audit managers. He is clearly seduced by their cynicism about the packaged messages distributed at the conference, just as Andrew was in the previous story. Both of them find that their simple pride of belonging to the enterprise is soon undermined. But there is an invisible line beyond which 'acceptable' criticism may not go; once crossed, a heavy bureaucratic response is invited – because the criticism embarrasses or threatens senior officers in the organization. So satirizing the company's greed was a message which punctured the 'client first' rhetoric. The severe response from top management suggests that the sentiment quite likely contained more than a grain of truth. One symptom of a divided and uneasy organization is the extent to which the less powerful will relish such occurrences, while attempts at suppression will tend to backfire. It is as if such organizations need a little scandal to relieve the frustrations of those who feel unhappy or aggrieved with their lot. Even better if the gossip is aimed at the pompous or powerful.

Finally, the accoutrements of the presentational event in the story are worthy of note – grand food, upbeat music and swish presentational aids. These can be viewed as expensive extravagances. But such devices are employed to inculcate more positive feelings along with the message content. 'Light' feelings of awe and delight tend to increase people's susceptibility to a 'cause'; they feel more comfortable and relaxed. They also feel that, as members of organizations, they can afford and enjoy luxuries and grandeur beyond their private means. In this manner, more and more organizations try to engineer a passion or enthusiasm for their values, mission or products. They have learned what evangelical missionaries and pop group impresarios have known for some time – that public events can do this, but they require careful stage managing.

Bill's Story: The Leaving Dinner

My leaving meal was first mentioned after a presentation I had done. The director of our department, with whom I had previous little contact, gave me a 'reassuring' nod, said the presentation was excellent, and how he'd always thought I was shy. He then said he'd have to organize a leaving dinner for me – 'Do you like Chinese?'

*A few weeks later I was approached by Stephanie, his secretary, about giving her a list of names of people I would like to invite. '***Obviously***', I was told, 'my Mentor, the director and the training manager would go'. As she zoomed off into the distance I wondered how many people I could invite? I didn't want to be greedy, but then again I didn't want to leave anyone out. Also, there were those you felt obliged to invite and those you really wanted to invite. Luckily these two corresponded for me, but there were also two girls from another department who had been really kind to me and I had gone out socially with them during my placement. It was always those two who had helped me with the silly little, but important, things that you would never dream of asking your boss about.*

I returned later in the day with my list which seemed three times longer than I had anticipated. I immediately felt I was taking advantage of the situation and reacted by babbling on about how I wasn't sure how many people I should invite, or whether I should just stick to people in our department. Stephanie thought I should, so we proceeded to cross my two friends off the list.

*On entering the restaurant I spotted the group sat in the corner. One member stuck out – he was not on my list – my sacred list! He was from our department. It wasn't that I didn't like him; it was just that there was no reason why he should be there – ***and*** he was taking the place of Amanda and Susan.*

This incident, and the rest of the evening, confirmed my existing awareness of the competitiveness of the department within the company. It also highlighted a fact that I had not previously been aware of – the cliquishness and competitiveness within the department. The company had restructured just before I joined, and had changed from a regional to a centralized one. I was based at the new Head Office.

As the evening meal progressed, and the stories poured out, it became evident that all of them had previously worked in the old Northern Region and they were all connected in some way. Gossip, scandals and 'in jokes' were tumbling out about people within the department, within other departments, and individuals fairly senior to the company. Some of the jokes and comments, although laughed off in this situation, were extremely rude and insulting. One of the main reasons for centralizing was to pool together the

*resources and team effort. Fierce competition between the regions
had caused considerable loss to the company as a whole. Here,
however, was a situation whereby the old regional group still
remained within the department, and a new form of competition
was evolving between the departments and sectors.*

*Although everyone was relaxed during and after the meal, when
I first arrived the atmosphere was a bit strained. They were all sat
huddled in the corner, looking awkward in their casual clothes,
stripped of the confidence and supremacy they had in the office. It
had always been me, in my suit in the surroundings of the air
conditioned office, that had felt awkward and out of place. In the
restaurant it was they who seemed uncomfortable, like fish out of
water. That's strange, because we were really in 'neutral' territory.
It took me a while to get used to the director sat there in his
trainers, open neck shirt and choker, telling dirty jokes and
discussing people. In a way I felt disappointed with him; but in
another way relieved. I was disappointed that he was gossiping
about people in his department but relieved that he was just
ordinary, like everyone else. I now not only saw him as **the
director** but as an ordinary individual to whom I could relate.
Funnily enough, next day at work I felt totally different from
usual. More confident and more relaxed.*

The apparently simple job of arranging a farewell dinner acts as a
catalyst to expose a whole range organizational motifs – most of
which the student has been unaware of. When we go about our
jobs, fixed in orbit by our roles, work relationships have a
structured predictability, following routinized scripts which help
get the work done. An unusual social event shakes all this. A rite
of passage out of the organization, as in the present case, raises
questions about legitimacy (Who should join? Who should not be
offended?) and self-presentation (What should I wear? Is this
work or play?). It tests boundaries (Am I the honoured person who
runs the party or am I a subordinate following instructions?).

Bill stumbled through this process, but experienced workers
have similar problems. At times the protocol can become more
important than the desires of the main celebrant – a little like
weddings which are structured more for social appearances than
for the pleasure of the bride and bridegroom. Above all, the formal
organizational status of possible participants has to be respected.
Indeed, Bill's junior status did not even give him the right to
invite people he really wanted with him at 'his' dinner. Functions

and celebrations then involve certain contradictions: between the equality, collegiality and friendship of the participants and a reaffirmation of differences of status and power; or between a relaxation of bureaucratic rules and the placing of invisible thresholds of appropriate behaviour.

Our view about colleagues or bosses is often taken from the roles we see them play in work-related exchanges. Unless they are also personal friends, out-of-workplace encounters can feel awkward or embarrassing, generating considerable amounts of anxiety. The usual trappings of status, work-role behaviours and dress have gone, so what can you talk about? How intimate or familiar can we become with colleagues, subordinates and superiors? All at Bill's parting dinner were fazed for a little while. For Bill, it was disconcerting to observe the physical and psychological transformation of his colleagues. But the experience also added value to his working relationships, demystifying the director – he was no god after all, just an ordinary guy. Such events point to the different personae, or 'masks', that we exchange as we move from one social setting to the next, and reveal how limited our knowledge and trust of people with whom we work can be. Some people are more adept than others at switching masks.

Thinking On

1 Think of functions or ceremonies organized by your school, university or employer. What do they now tell you about the outward image the organization wished to portray?
2 Should we have more, or fewer, rites of passage in organizations? What do they achieve?
3 What do you feel when you meet someone out of their normal work role? What accounts for your feelings?
4 Andrew and Mark were both exposed to an intense dose of 'company values' – and both ended up disenchanted. Why? Is this inevitable?
5 Imagine you have to organize a really effective conference to convince fellow students – some known to be reluctant joiners – to work together to help a major charity build a sanctuary for the homeless in your local town. You have a fair bit of money for the event. How would you make it work?

Reading On

The purpose and value of ceremonies as rites of passage have long
been of interest to anthropologists studying different cultures,
and communities – see especially Trice and Beyer (1984) and
Kuper (1977). These works show the way people ritualize and
celebrate important social transitions in their communities, such
as a birth, death or a change in leadership. Writers such as
Isabella (1990) and Czarniawska-Joerges (1992) reveal how
major shifts and consolidations in work organizations are also
marked by rites of passage – they facilitate the questioning and
destruction of an established order and the enhancement of a new
one.

Functions and ceremonies are intimately connected with the
symbols and symbolism of organizational culture – its management, change and control. A good background text is offered by
Andrew Brown (1995). Brown provides a comprehensive analysis
of organizational culture, highlighting the often vivid mark of
some corporate ceremonies in reinforcing the cultural values –
akin to acts of cultural worship. Brown discusses the way
functions and ceremonies can contribute to organizational
change, although there are more specialist texts in this area –
such as Bate (1994), Frost et al. (1991) and Schein (1985).
Schein's work has been particularly influential in that it carefully
distinguishes ceremonies – a relatively superficial manifestation
of an organization's culture – from deeper, less obvious, 'value'
influences on an organization's culture.

Case studies and ethnographies of how specific corporations
manage culture and its ceremonies are revealing for their fine
details and subtleties – more of the sort of data reported in this
chapter. A good example is Kunda's (1992) meticulous observations of the social fabric of a high technology engineering
organization. Peters and Waterman (1982) identify the details of
the ceremonies and rituals of major corporations that seem to
contribute to organizational success – at least for a period of time.

Bate, P. (1994). *Strategies for Cultural Change*. Oxford: Butterworth Heine-
    mann.
Brown, A. (1995). *Organisational Culture*. London: Pitman.
Czarniawska-Joerges, B. (1992). *Exploring Complex Organizations*. Newbury
    Park, CA: Sage.
Frost, P.J., Moore, L.F., Louis, M.R., Lundberg, C.C. and Martin, J. (eds) (1991).
    Reframing Organizational Culture. Newbury Park, CA: Sage.

Isabella, L.A. (1990). 'Evolving interpretations as a change unfolds: how managers construe key organizational events', *Academy of Management Journal*, 33, 1, 7–41.

Kunda, G. (1992). *Engineering Culture: Control and Commitment in a High-tech Corporation*. Philadelphia, PA: Temple University Press.

Kuper, A. (1977). *Anthropology and Anthropologists*. London: Routledge and Kegan Paul.

Peters, T. and Waterman, R.H. (1982). *In Search of Excellence*. New York: Warner.

Schein, E. (1985). *Organizational Culture and Leadership*. San Francisco, CA: Jossey-Bass.

Trice, H.M. and Beyer, J.M. (1984). 'Studying organizational cultures through rites and ceremonials', *American Management Review*, 9, 653–69.

5

The Gods

To many people in the lower echelons of organizations, top leaders are the object of acute curiosity, fascination and gossip. This is especially so when we rarely catch sight of them, and then only on ceremonial occasions. A physical and psychological gulf seems to separate top leaders from ordinary organizational members, who often fantasize about their leaders. In these fantasies, leaders can feature in different ways – as benevolent, father-like figures, as demonic schemers engaged in plotting and machination, as cunning wheeler-dealers who strike clever deals for the organization, as impostors who attained their position by deception, and so forth.

The innocent eyes of young trainees can capture admirably some of the qualities, both good and bad, which are projected onto leaders. Most older, seasoned members of organizations would find it embarrassing discussing such notions with others. Trainees can also write very lucidly about their own feelings when they finally get to meet these distant figures upon whom so much is seen to depend.

Anna, a Greek trainee, tells her story first. She speaks in terms of a religious experience when she finally got to meet the Director of a Greek publishing company, for whom she worked.

Anna's Story: The Most Precious Experience of my Placement

Is it really possible to capture the essence of an organization through a single event? This sounds quite scary, though it is a pretty attractive idea. For three or four days now, my mind has been travelling back to Athens, where I had my placement, trying to revive my working life and experiences. I remember people being stressed, running up and down in their offices, preparing themselves for meetings, people being happy or sad, people chatting or working non-stop.

I can remember my first day at work. My brother accompanied me to the office. I was literally shaking! I also remember the last day at work. I think that this is going to remain vividly in my memory. I was sad. All the people in the department were sad also. I wanted this day to last longer than usual. People were coming to wish me goodbye and kept asking me when I will be back.

There is indeed so much to write about and thus it is very confusing to try and select just one thing to refer to. Yet, after a lot of thinking, I have decided on something that truly deserves to be written down. It is probably the most precious experience that I had during my placement.

Working was something new for me as this was the first time I worked for a firm other than my Dad's. This was 'proper' work for the first time. As most people do when they find themselves in a new environment, I kept on observing and thinking. I was analysing people's actions and reactions, attitudes and overall behaviour. Everybody seemed to have his/her own role, every department its own aims and its own functions. The theories we had learned at the university, about roles, hierarchy, working groups, etc., seemed to come alive right in front of my eyes, leaving me satisfied and even more interested in the subject of my studies. But what about this 'myth' of management? What is the top person's role in all that? What is it to lead people? These were the questions that I needed the answers for. After much wondering, I decided to try and have a discussion with my top manager, a conversation which would, hopefully, help me to solve the 'mystery'.

As the manager was extremely busy for days and days, I was becoming even more obsessed with the idea that I had to talk with her and ask her to reveal to me all the secrets that had guided her to success. Finally one afternoon she was free and pleased to talk to me. I then realized for a moment that my request was difficult. I wanted to find out about **everything***. Was this feasible? I explained most of my thoughts to her, she understood all the worries that had been in my mind all this time. We discussed a lot of things involving managerial concepts and attitudes.*

The first issue was that of managerial style, in particular the ways in which a manager imposes him or herself on his or her subordinates. Can one win the trust of others by fear or by personal respect? The answer was respect. If you have knowledge of the work subject, and if what you want is the involvement and cooperation of your subordinates, then you have found a sure way to get what you want from your department. A successful manager must first of all have passion for his or her work. This is the basis for transmitting your personal enthusiasm to the people you are working with and to inspire them to work with you to reach the organizational targets.

A manager should try to analyse each one of his or her subordinates and aim for a better understanding, better cooperation and finally positive results. By making a correct use of the abilities and the talents of each one, we help them set feasible goals that benefit the whole department, and enable them to succeed at a personal level as well.

*A good manager must also be **accessible** to his or her subordinates in both business and personal terms. People are indeed the most important issue within the organization and the art of handling them should be one of the major abilities a manager should be endowed with. Nobody starts his or her career as manager. And if this is the case, they are bound to fail. Only by understanding and considering the position of a subordinate – this is by taking his or her place at least once – can the management of the people and the department be fair and effective.*

The discussion continued for a long time and all the issues were mainly connected with the human aspect of the organization. My satisfaction from listening to my manager talk about these issues was indescribable. All these theories, which I had seen applied in our department with great success, were now reconfirmed to me by my manager, a person whom I respect and admire enormously. I consider myself very lucky to have worked as a subordinate for this particular manager. I hope that one day I will have the chance to practice all that I have learned and I am still learning, becoming a successful manager.

What made Anna's meeting with the senior manager of her organization 'the most precious experience' of her six-month placement? Talking to someone successful, someone who confirmed the value of her academic learning as a launching pad for a career in management, was evidently very important. However, her 'indescribable' satisfaction appears to be out of proportion with the views on management which she describes, views which would strike some more cynical commentators as pious platitudes. Yet, the very fervour with which she reports these views provides strong evidence that the commonplace can sound extraordinary, and clichés can sound like wisdom when uttered by 'great' leaders.

Anna's manager was portrayed as an inspirational leader. She was someone Anna not only 'respected and admired enormously', but a person with whom she could identify – a role model. This manager was to be emulated; a successful woman in a business culture dominated by men. The fact that this apparently outstanding woman took the time to talk to Anna in person, to address her worries and answer her questions, is important. It is perhaps not accidental that Anna emphasizes how 'extremely busy' her manager had been prior to the meeting, nor that she sees accessibility as an important attribute of good managers. Anna's vivid description of her own nervousness before the eagerly-anticipated meeting, as well as her feeling of relief that her manager had understood 'all her worries' in a flash, suggest the centrality of her manager in her own emotional life. The manager seems almost as important to her as an object of love.

Anna's account highlights a theme of innumerable organizational stories and fantasies, in which one comes face to face with the Big Boss. This theme assumes numerous forms. In Anna's story, meeting the Big Boss serves to reaffirm her faith in her studies and in her chosen career. In other accounts, meeting the Big Boss reaffirms faith in the organization's goals, in oneself or in humanity itself – the boss himself or herself turns out to be a real person. In yet other accounts, meeting the Big Boss leads to disappointment and disillusionment. This is a dominant motif of the following incident told by Kim. Kim worked for a retail outlet, famed for its democratic principles.

Kim's Story: Time Need Not be Wasted on Lesser Mortals

Six months in a national retail organization. OK, so it's not a City firm and it's not everyone's idea of a high flying business, but it seemed to offer what I thought I was after, at a wage that couldn't be laughed at.

I went to work with few preconceived ideas and no experience. Although the organization turned out to be run like a military camp and was a complete shock to me socially and culturally, I just about managed to keep my head above water. As far as I was concerned, my placement had been a success, that is until I had a parting chat with the Managing Director of the branch. Much of my confidence in management and the organization collapsed when I went to see the 'Boss'. The event that discoloured my opinion appears to sum up a classic syndrome afflicting many senior managers: 'Time need not be wasted on lesser mortals'. Scathing generalization I know, yet in this case very relevant.

My conversation with the boss took the following course:

'Right, you've been here for long?'
'Five months to date.'
'And you've come from a poly?'
'No, from a university, Bath University.'
'And this is part of your degree?'
'Yes, I am studying for a degree in Business Administration.'
'And what has your placement with us consisted of?'
'Basically I have had a fairly comprehensive insight into the company, spending time in several different departments. I have covered both the administrative and shop-floor departments.'
'Right, and have we been paying you for this?'
'Yes.'
'And how much is that?'
'£9,500 per year.'
'And when are you leaving?'
'This Saturday.'
'And do you return here on your next placement?'
'It's not compulsory so I will probably try and be placed in a City firm.'

It was in this style that the conversation went on. He had obviously not bothered to spend even five minutes going over my file, and hence spent the whole time asking what he should have already known. Although I was only a small cog in the machine, the impression he made upon me in those ten minutes was to be damaging to both him and the organization that he represented. His inability to review my situation and relate to me reflected badly, not only upon himself but upon the company.

Having been so scathing about the MD, I do realize that he had very limited time, and probably more pressing engagements. And although this incident should not reflect on the corporation as a whole, my instinctive inclination, and to a certain extent my naïveté, meant that my opinion of the branch and its management had collapsed. In my view, it does not say much that a senior manager could not be bothered to find out about the subject in hand, and appeared so unprepared.

My main thought on this incident is that certain managers

within the company, and probably in other organizations, do not respect their subordinates, nor do they realize that it is the lesser mortals that account for the running of such businesses.

Kim's account reveals that meeting the Big Boss can be a disillusioning experience, just as easily as it can be exhilarating and inspiring. Her boss agreed to meet her, but then 'neglected' to prepare himself for the meeting. Instead of providing the crowning glory to her placement, it turns into an anti-climax. Would it not have been simpler to delegate the parting formalities to a 'less busy' or more socially adept subordinate? What Kim sensed was the boss's double presumption; first, he presumed that no briefing was necessary for such a meeting, and second, that the student should feel grateful about being allowed to meet him. The incident reveals the emotional vulnerability of the subordinate when meeting a highly powerful and prestigious person. Kim does not claim that the Director intended to insult her, yet the discussion of her feelings indicates that an unintentional slight is no less hurtful than an intended one.

Anna's and Kim's stories highlight the fundamental asymmetry in many leader–follower relationships. Both happy and sad stories centring on meetings with the top leader suggest that there is often a gulf – emotional, social and psychological – between leaders and their subordinates which may, or may not, be bridgeable. Leaders meet many, sometimes hundreds or thousands, of their members in the course of their work. Shaking hands with the boss may be a unique experience for an employee; a leader, however, will shake numerous hands every day. It can be hard to make every handshake meaningful and warm, even with the knowledge that it may be the other person's only handshake with him or her.

The follower will usually know the name of the organization's leader, will be able to recognize his or her face from photographs, may know his or her likes and dislikes from press reports, interviews and gossip as well as knowing where the leader lives and what car he or she drives. The leader, on the other hand, will probably not know the names of the majority of his or her followers, their faces will be virtually indistinguishable from those of members of any other organization, and their likes and dislikes are virtually immaterial. The essential difference between Anna's and Kim's stories is that whereas Anna's boss bridged the gulf, making her feel valued and respected, Kim's boss (probably unknowingly) used the parting ritual to underline the status and power distance which separated them. In doing so he alienated a potential employee by leaving her with a negative image of the organization.

Why is meeting the organization's leader such an important event in people's emotional lives? Why does it feature in many of the organizational stories? As we argued earlier, people in organizations spend much time fantasizing about their leaders. Meeting the boss tests these fantasies, positively reinforcing some, derailing others. Anna's story is built around the notion that the leader will provide her with the inspiration and reassurance she needs in order to continue her studies, while Kim's story, more obliquely, touches on the expectation that a leader will recognize her from among the numerous trainees employed by his firm. Kim's leader will address her as a worthy member of the organization, if not as his equal.

One of the most common images, or auras, generated by organizational leaders is that of omnipotence. This is often consciously sustained by the leaders themselves, though followers tend to project truly exceptional powers onto them. Yet a potent type of experience, spawning numerous stories and myths, centres on the discovery that leaders are only human. They too are afraid and they also may be driven by someone standing above them. This realization can be highly unsettling, cutting an idol down to size. Alternatively, it can be liberating – fallible, confused leaders are less fearful to behold if they, in their turn, sit in awe of their own superiors.

The story which follows is recounted by Steve. It vividly describes some of the fantasies surrounding the top leadership of a famous transnational corporation. Steve tells how his faith in his own leader was shattered when he realized that he was just a puppet on someone else's string.

Steve's Story: The Day I Lost Faith in Mike McKie

Before discussing the incident in question, it is helpful to give a few details of the company. Although DACRO UK is an affiliate of DACRO International based in the US, it is officially a separate entity with its own management, culture and vision. DACRO UK is split into seven major product divisions, each of which functions independently of the others. The division to which I was assigned is called the Consumer Appliances Division (CAD) and deals in the traditional appliances. CAD is headed up by an executive named Mike McKie.

When I joined DACRO the demands on McKie appeared to come from two sources. I have already mentioned the US connection, but DACRO UK prided itself on its independence, its distinct culture and its ability to outperform its US parent company. If the British subsidiary's independence was genuine, McKie should be answerable to the demi-gods of DACRO UK (i.e. the Board of Directors). Perched on the twenty-first floor of DACRO House, these mythical creatures are reputed to rule from sumptuous quarters of mahogany and leather. Nobody you meet within the company has actually entered the twenty-first floor and nobody is quite sure what goes on there. However, most people have their own story of a personal encounter with Zeus himself – Erroll Bates, CEO of DACRO UK.

This report describes the events surrounding December 9, the day I lost faith in McKie. McKie had stressed on frequent occasions that CAD needed a radical change in structure in order to become more 'customer focused' – a condition he believed to be essential if DACRO were to remain successful in the 1990s. He had developed his own plans to this effect and had begun to implement some of them with considerable ceremony. However all these plans were laid to rest on December 9, when Peter Kellner, Head of CAD worldwide in Corporate Headquarters in Boston, announced his global strategy for change. DACRO UK senior management were told of the announcement a fortnight before the event. They spent two weeks anticipating what Kellner would announce and how his 'decree' would affect CAD UK. Indeed they were so anxious, that they arranged a satellite link-up with the US so that they could listen to Kellner 'live'. However, there was little or no communication between senior management and the rest of the workforce during this period. The workforce sensed how significant the announcement was to senior management and began to speculate on what it would mean for the future of DACRO UK – negative rumour was rife. Incredibly, management did absolutely nothing *to dispel these rumours: they must have known what scenarios were being discussed and yet they stuck their heads in the sand and pretended that it was business as usual.*

December 9 came to pass and Kellner made his speech. His 'grand design' was swallowed hook, line and sinker – and McKie has made changes in line with the 'edict' ever since. No consideration has been given to the possible culture differences and market disparities between the US and the UK, or any attempt to 'interpret' the edict in line with the strategy of DACRO UK. In fact, McKie completely disregarded his own strategy for the future of the division and appears to have adopted enthusiastically Kellner's plans in their entirety.

*Initially, I had a lot of time and respect for McKie. He was (in my mind) an unsuccessful [sic] executive who would in time turn CAD and around by adhering to his principles and 'sticking it out'. He was very much a 'people' manager with a high profile – always encouraging, and seeing the silver lining in every cloud. All my preconceptions were shattered by the events of and around December 9. The way McKie and his management team acqui-esced to Kellner's announcement was spineless. Why didn't McKie have the guts to continue with **his** strategy for the UK? The sudden change in vision and direction was detrimental to the division's morale and devastating to McKie's authority. Kellner had made the call and McKie had jumped. During the weeks preceding December 9, McKie frequently scurried off to Boston, presumably to ingratiate himself with US senior management (this only served to alienate him further from his UK workforce). I com-pletely lost faith in his authority because it became so second-hand in my eyes. I also experienced a feeling of vulnerability as an employee. The security that a strong management provides had been removed – the UK management team appeared to lack the guts to lead – it was as if they would stick their heads in a fire at the whim of the US.*

Perhaps more important was the impact on morale. Manage-ment did not effectively communicate with the rest of the workforce in any shape or form. We were sent one communiqué outlining what was happening on December 9, 'a critical announcement which may result in radical changes within CAD'. That was all the information which we were given and so we were left to speculate what these changes might involve. Many scenarios evolved, and, human nature being what it is, these inevitably included much doom and gloom: massive job cuts and reshuffling were the favourite elements in most prophecies. Consequently for a week leading up to the announcement morale at work plummeted. The atmosphere became polluted by fear and suspicion. CAD has been going through difficult times recently but until this incident the management still enjoyed the support of those under them. However their complete disregard for anybody other than them-selves over this affair really lowered the esteem in which they were held.

It would be worth mentioning that this incident was of much more significance to me than to others within the division. Those employees who had been with the company for a while had perhaps come to terms with the fact that their senior management were little more than puppets of Boston. However, because I was new to the company, I felt 'let down'. Initially, I had almost idolized the executives at DACRO UK, and when my image of them was shattered I became bitter and resentful. To cope with my feelings, I found myself turning my attention away from the UK senior management team towards the US for signs of where the company was heading. Directives which were endorsed by Boston became highly significant, while those of UK origin I dismissed as petty.

Finally, it is worth pointing out how the whole affair destroyed the 'magic' of the twenty-first floor myth. I had adopted the fantasy that surrounded Bates and the directors and it had become a form of motivation to think of these overseers controlling operations. However the implication of the Kellner affair is that Bates and his Board are little more than figureheads, with no real power or purpose. This realization filled me with disillusion and the twenty-first floor became quite a pathetic spectacle.

Steve's story gets to the heart of the emotional bond between leader and follower in large organizations. It vividly depicts the great powers with which leaders are endowed in their followers' eyes, and also the disturbing consequences resulting from the discovery that they are fallible after all. Leaders who inspired faith, commitment and awe are relegated to mere mortals and become targets for extraordinary hostility and contempt. Discovering that the leader is not omnipotent undermines his or her perceived capacity to protect the subordinates and to stand up for them. The leader's weakness makes the followers feel vulnerable and exposed. It also leaves them feeling betrayed, as if they had placed their trust in a false prophet.

Why do subordinates use such harsh standards when judging leaders? Why do they build them up to such heights that they can only come crashing down? Why can they not treat leaders as ordinary mortals, just like themselves? Doubtless many leaders connive in the mystique which surrounds them, by isolating themselves on the 'twenty-first floor' and in executive suites, wearing masks of unshakeable certainty and conviction and eschewing most normal traces of humility, doubt or hesitation. Believing that no one wants weak leaders, they equate macho qualities with strong leadership. Yet even leaders who choose to mix with the troops, like McKie, are attributed with powers that are totally out of proportion to their actual position or personal qualities.

Why? Maybe we find it hard to imagine the huge and famous organizations which dominate our society, the organizations whose logos, products and advertisements become deeply entrenched in our minds, being run by ordinary humans like ourselves. Is it possible that, in our minds, only very remarkable people, quite unlike us, can manage organizations like IBM, Shell and Toyota? Do the prestige and might of these corporate empires call for the demi-gods as featured in Steve's story? Perhaps so. However, Steve's reactions contain an important psychological truth. It is difficult to accept the idea that we are working for an organization led by nonentities. Leaders must be endowed with superhuman qualities because only then can they really be perceived as real leaders – to be accepted and respected.

Thinking On

1   What fuels the curiosities of organizational members about their leaders?
2   What fantasies have you ever had about individuals in leadership positions, like headmasters, directors or even politicians and statespeople?
3   Have you ever had an experience of meeting an important leader? What memories have you preserved of such meetings? What do these memories reveal about your bond with such leaders?
4   Would Anna's glowing feeling towards her director persist, if she stayed with the organization much longer?
5   Do you think that Kim reacted in an over-sensitive way to the director's lack of briefing? Is it reasonable to expect a very busy person to be personally briefed about every one of the subordinates he or she is likely to meet?
6   Should Steve reconcile himself to the fact that leaders, even top leaders of powerful organizations, have their limitations and that their actions are often driven by ignoble, short-sighted or confused motives? How might he respond if he were to meet Kellner in his next industrial placement?

Reading on

While leadership has attracted much attention, 'followership' does not feature so prominently in academic literature. Tolstoy's

War and Peace, however, provides singularly perceptive psychological portraits of the feelings subordinates harbour towards their leaders, both positive and negative. Burns' (1978) classic study goes a long way to establishing the connections between effective leadership and the psychological needs of subordinates, and distinguishes between transformational and transactional leaders. The former articulate their followers' needs and present them with ways of fulfilling them, the latter improve organizational performance by striking clever deals and getting things effectively organized. This distinction has been the basis for contrasting leaders with managers, as proposed by Zaleznik (1977). Bennis (1989) and Bennis and Nanus (1985) have argued that leaders do the 'right things' while managers 'do things right'.

There are studies of how subordinates incorporate leaders into their fantasy lives, projecting onto them qualities which were once identified with parents and other figures of authority. Relevant writers are Bryman (1986, 1992), Bion (1961), Levinson (1972), Kohut (1976), Kets de Vries (1990), Kets de Vries and Miller (1984) and Hirschhorn (1988). Most of these build on the work of Freud (1921) who explored the role of the leader in group processes. He noted that many groups are held together by the members' shared identification with the leader; this identification displays qualities similar to both being in love and being under hypnosis. Building on Freud's and Kohut's work on leadership and Max Weber's concept of charismatic leadership, Lindholm (1988) has detailed many features of the leadership–follower relation, including idealization – the similarities between devotion to a leader and being in love.

The leaders' own delusions and their catastrophic effects on performance of military organizations are admirably captured by Dixon (1976). An extended interpretation and discussion of the narratives in this chapter can be found in Gabriel (1997).

Bennis, W. (1989). *Why Leaders can't Lead. The Unconscious Conspiracy Continues*. San Francisco, CA: Jossey-Bass.

Bennis, W.G. and Nanus, B. (1985). *Leaders: The Strategies for Taking Charge*. New York: Harper and Row.

Bion, W.R. (1961). *Experiences in Groups*. London: Tavistock.

Bryman, A. (1986). *Leadership and Organizations*. London: Routledge and Kegan Paul.

Bryman, A. (1992). *Charisma and Leadership in Organizations*. London: Sage.

Burns, J.M. (1978). *Leadership*. New York: Harper and Row.

Dixon, N.F. (1976). *On the Psychology of Military Incompetence*. London: Jonathan Cape.

Freud, S. (1921). *Group Psychology and the Analysis of the Ego* (Standard Edn). London: Hogarth Press.

Gabriel, Y. (1997). 'Meeting God: when organizational members come face to face with the supreme leader', *Human Relations*, in press.

Hirschhorn, L. (1988). *The Workplace Within*. Cambridge, MA: MIT Press.

Kets de Vries, M.F.R. (1990). 'The organizational fool: balancing a leader's hubris', *Human Relations*, 43, 8, 751–70.

Kets de Vries, M.F.R. and Miller, D. (1984). *The Neurotic Organization*. San Francisco, CA: Jossey-Bass.

Kohut, H. (1976). 'Creativity, charisma, and group psychology', in J.E. Gedo and G.H. Pollock (eds), *Freud: The Fusion of Science and Humanism*. New York: International Universities Press.

Levinson, H. (1972). *Organizational Diagnosis*. Cambridge, MA: Harvard University Press.

Lindholm, C. (1988). 'Lovers and leaders: a comparison of social and psychological models of romance and charisma', *Social Science Information*, 27, 1, 3–45.

Zaleznik, A. (1977). 'Managers and leaders: are they different?', *Harvard Business Review*, 55, May–June, 66–77.

PART 2

WINNING AND LOSING

'Winning is not everything!' used to be a cornerstone of liberal education. Games were for fun, for building character, for learning to respect the rules and the verdict of the referee. The view that games are about participation, about doing your best, and showing magnanimity in victory and grace in defeat seems rather old-fashioned today. Occasionally, gallant losers in sport may still attract some admiration or sympathy. In today's 'executive success game', however, only victory counts. This is a message to which student trainees become quickly attuned.

Competition has always been at the heart of capitalism – competition for customers, for profits, for innovation and for products. As companies struggle for survival, they have always sought to outgrow and outperform their competitors. What is different about today's organizations seems to be the sense that business is *only* about winning; every day appears to be a fighting day, in which battles are won and lost, reputations are made and destroyed, alliances are struck and broken, opponents are out-manoeuvred, neutralized or defeated. The very vocabulary of business has been invaded by military terminology – strategy (the art of generalship), tactics, raids, targets, penetration, outflanking, ambushes, predators, sieges, flak, piracy.

In such an environment, few things count for more than the reputation of being a winner; a manager's greatest fear becomes that of being labelled a loser. This is the main link between Part 1 and Part 2 of this book. Being seen as a winner is not merely the outcome of success, but also the result of self-promotion and publicity. It is an attempt to be a step ahead of others and a determination to treat every transaction as a game of winning and losing. The trappings of accomplishment – the cars, the offices, the salary – are themselves objects of continuous wrangling. They are a visible set of criteria attesting the power and status of an individual.

Based on a study of 250 American executives, Michael Maccoby has argued:

A new type of man is taking over the leadership of the most technically advanced companies in America. In contrast to the jungle-fighter industrialists of the past, he is driven not to build or to preside over empires, but to organize winning teams. Unlike the security-seeking organization man, he is excited by the chance to cut deals and to gamble. (1976: 34)

But corporate gamesmanship is not limited to the highest echelons of organizations. Every office and every shop-floor becomes an arena where individuals compete for money, status and, to an extent, jobs. Corporate gamesmanship involves a constantly shifting network of alliances and factions, loyalties and intrigues. It also involves opportunism – the ability to make maximum use of openings that come one's way, to cultivate potentially useful contacts and to redefine friends and enemies according to expedience. These are the major ingredients of the stories in this part of the book.

Reference

Maccoby, Michael. (1976). *The Gamesman: New Corporate Leaders*. New York: Simon and Schuster.

6

Winners and Losers

The image of an organization in which everyone collaborates towards a common objective has always been a popular feature of management rhetoric. Teamwork is an often-extolled virtue of an organization in which everyone is meant to pull together – to sink or to swim together. Yet the organizational world, as it emerges from the accounts of trainees, is a far cry from this. Competition, overt or covert, conflict and antagonism capture their attention with far greater vividness and regularity than cooperation. While some of the competition is between departments, it more frequently focuses on individuals.

Some of the accounts provided by new recruits paint organizations in dark colours. Incidents displaying the less worthy human attributes are recounted: ruthlessness, deception, backstabbing, indifference to others, arrogance and conceit. Lives at work are nasty and brutish. In the last few years, following waves of managerial sackings, careers have become short as well. In this world, there are few winners and many losers. Every man or woman stands for himself or herself.

The first story focuses on an archetypical 'yuppy', a highly successful executive, working for a firm of City merchant bankers. Geoff, the narrator, creates a vivid image of a man, whose 'doormat' he found himself to be. The story becomes especially poignant following the collapse of major banks in the 1990s.

Geoff's Story: A Winner's Portrait

Many people hold stereotypical views of the merchant banking environment – arrogant, power-crazed men, working long hours under intense pressures for vast sums of money, burnt-out after short careers. My personal experience after a six-month placement for Leber's has not dispelled these images.

I worked under Paul, a thirty-year-old bachelor on a rumoured salary of over £200,000 p.a. A red Porsche, a yacht and a flat in Barbican, which he shared with his cat, supported the rumours. I was often required to do personal favours for my boss, which extended beyond work practices, and the following was one such favour. He rang me at work one Friday afternoon from Zurich to ask me to 'run' his car to Heathrow, so he could travel straight from the airport to visit some friends in Cornwall. He felt it would be inconvenient to take a train back to his house first to pick up his car. I was told I could take a taxi back to work. The incident highlighted some fundamental aspects of the organization, its managers and its culture.

The first striking feature of this incident was the way it highlighted the power structure. Although the bank has a fairly flat hierarchy, managers never hesitated to make their position known by putting me in a position where I could not refuse (mind you, I actually quite fancied driving his Rover 8 series top model, the Porsche being explicitly out of bounds for me).

The organization's wasteful nature and disregard for the value of money are also revealed. The £47 taxi fare was put on the Leber's account. Although the organization appreciates making money, there is a total lack of cost consciousness. To many, money is no object. I suppose that £47 is pennies compared to a £47m takeover deal. The incident also showed disregard for my own time; it meant that I had to work unpaid overtime in order to catch up with my work (and on a Friday night!).

To say I was used as a doormat would be an understatement. Paul thrived on his feelings of domination. It seemed utterly unnecessary to have me drive his car to the airport. This attitude was common among management and it led to resentment and back-stabbing which could be seen at all levels of the organization. The incident did no harm to Paul's ego. Many managers, like him, were status and empire-builders showing extraordinary presumptuousness and arrogance. When asking me to drive his car, Paul classed the task as a 'small' favour – in fact it took me all afternoon. It is characteristic that, when speaking to me on the phone, Paul called me 'Geoffrey', as always, although I am known to all else as 'Geoff'. He likewise insists on calling his secretary Suzanne, although her name is Su and is printed as such on her birth certificate.

When I asked Paul on the phone about flight details and the whereabouts of the keys, his answer was 'My secretary has the details', although she had not. I don't think that Paul ever realized or cared about the embarrassing situation he put me in, when the rest of the office found out that I had become his personal chauffeur.

I had to go to Paul's house in order to pick up the car (I was under strict instructions not to take the Porsche, although it was very tempting). I was amazed when I entered his flat. It was completely unfurnished except for the kitchen, a study (with an ashtray full of cigar stubs – obviously the pressure) and a bedroom. The bedroom was full of shirts, ties, suits, but no other clothes. This emphasised how much work had taken over his life.

At the airport, I left a note with his car keys saying that I had enjoyed driving his car. When Paul came back to the office on Monday, he told me and his colleagues how, on seeing the note, he had been convinced that I had driven the Porsche. He seriously could not comprehend how I could enjoy driving a car 'such as a Rover', said in a jeering voice. I think this final twist summarizes how unable he is to comprehend anyone else apart from people like himself. This attitude is reflective of the whole organization, its managerial style and culture.

Geoff's story contrasts the aura of power in Paul's work life with the arid spaces of his personal life. It highlights the arrogance of power and money which Paul exemplifies, but which, in Geoff's eyes, is typical of the entire organization. This arrogance is expressed in numerous ways, large and small, from his indifference to other people's time and effort to his cavalier attitude to work expenses. He asks for 'favours' though he does not reciprocate them. He does not deign to give details which would save others considerable trouble. He does not mind if the entire office knows that he can treat Geoff as his errand boy.

Even his penchant for altering people's names reinforces the idea that he feels he can manipulate people, treating them the way that he wishes. People can be sensitive about their names – and with good reason. The way we are addressed is an immediate indicator of our status and esteem, as well as a marker of the relation we have with the person who addresses us. 'Paul', 'The Director', 'Ms' or 'Professor' are important signs which anchor our communication, establishing classes and categories of persons and relations. Mispronouncing someone's name can be an eccentric affectation, a sign of affection and familiarity or, as Geoff clearly sees it, an insult as if to emphasize that even his name can be manipulated as Paul pleases.

Geoff compares Paul's ability to do as he pleases in his business realm to the flat's emptiness – a sign of isolation, hollowness and decay. The very trappings of Paul's success – the Porsche, the yacht – underline his emotional isolation. Paul is an organizational

winner, there can be no doubt about this, yet Geoff has already
sketched a scenario which may turn him into a loser.

Geoff gives a highly perceptive account of his own feelings
towards Paul. He loathes being cast in the role of errand boy,
resents Paul's presumptuousness and despises his hauteur. Yet,
while not saying a single word in favour of Paul, he confesses to
getting a kick from the prospect of driving a fast car. Is there
perhaps a trace of envy, an aspiration to emulate Paul's success
one day, even if not his demeanour?

The next story is also one of contrasts. In it, Fay describes the
fate of winners and losers in a single day in the office of a regional
bus company.

Fay's Story: A Day in the Office

*I had worked with the marketing department for one month as a
member of one of four teams. John, a team manager from a
different team, was being promoted. On this day he received the
traditional send-off. Richard, our department head, had an
afternoon meeting and so the tribute was arranged for shortly
before lunch. It so happened that, on the same day, Richard had to
decide which of two female employees would be seconded indefi-
nitely to a different department. Neither wanted to go. In one
corner stood Jenny, my team manager, in the other stood Gill, a
supervisor in our team. The grapevine efficiently alerted everyone
to the forthcoming conflict and, as we prepared to honour John, a
state of tension rose in the office.*

*Tonia, a close friend of Jenny's, signalled everyone to stop work
and gather around. Attention focused on John, while Richard lit
his pipe and ceremoniously praised John's efforts and achieve-
ments. Everyone smiled, laughed and applauded handsomely. As
he looked upon us for the last time, John's speech on his days with
us was interrupted here and there by signs of his emotions.
Presents were exchanged, too, though the 'best' was saved till last.
Tonia and Jenny presented John with a life-size inflatable sheep,
complete with orifice. Richard was uncomfortable with the
lowered tone, but did not express his disapproval. John went more
scarlet than the ribbon around the sheep's neck.*

*Richard returned to his office and people resumed their activi-
ties. All except Jenny, who sneaked into Richard's office as the rest
of us dispersed. Gill sat at her desk. After a while Jenny
summoned her into Richard's office. Again tense, pretending to be*

working hard, we waited anxiously for the outcome. **Bang!** *The door slammed behind Jenny, who glanced around the department with a distinctly smug grin, then walked away, victorious. Gill came out and returned to her desk. She had lost her job. Jenny had won the fight. Gill sat crying with disappointment and hurt. Even the least sympathetic people understood. They knew the history of deliberate scapegoating carried out by Jenny. But Richard allowed it. He had been unable to see through it!*

Following this incident, I was given Gill's position of Corporate Hospitality Manager. This meant more challenge and responsibility. Yet, my part in the actual incident was that of an onlooker. I was conscious that I was not personally involved in the complex interrelationships, but did not realize how quickly I would become an integrated member of the group. Nor was I aware of how much insight I was absorbing. The organization rewarded intense work. John was one example of many middle managers who were hard working, so his promotion was well-deserved. But the company's senior management were so task-orientated that people were in positions of leadership without the necessary skills.

The marketing department, in particular, seemed to lack judgement over what personality types should join or lead our teams. Jenny promoted poor office behaviour by continuously contaminating her colleagues with crude gossip. Her aggressive management style intimidated other colleagues, and she pushed her way into knowing about everybody's projects. Her ability to be the first to let Richard in on 'her' information secured her tyranny. This, coupled with Richard's obvious weakness, meant that the department lacked positive leadership. Richard was not the man for the job. He may have understood buses, but he was not a leader. He was not a source of motivation or vision. In the incident he hides his weakness by following formal codes of speech behaviour. When it came to demoting Gill, he was either a man of bad judgement or very weak will. Gill actually possessed many admirable people leadership skills, but she was unable to guide us because Jenny used her superior formal authority to oppose Gill.

At the time of the incident, I felt shock at the company's unprofessionalism. I also felt despair for Gill, whom I admired. Yet this emotion conflicted with my own hopes that I might be promoted. Now, I feel familiarity, discussing a part of my own life, but I also feel guilt because of the negative things I have reported about these people. I feel guilty because I actually did enjoy my placement immensely and, after all, without these people and their problems I would not have learned half as much about office behaviour. As I was a fly on the wall to all these events I feel very lucky, but, in truth I would not want to work there.

In this diverse story, office politics are presented as a deadly game. John was a clear winner being promoted to greener pastures, though not before he had endured the ordeal of the sheep. On the same day, following speeches of gratitude and appreciation for John, Gill lost her 'hospitality' job, being left with an unclear future. Fay, our narrator, emerges as an unexpected winner, and who knows, maybe a villain too, in the eyes of others. Jenny had much to be cheerful about; she had got rid of a dangerous rival and had proven once more her ability to twist Richard round her little finger. Her 'tyranny' was set to continue. Fay sketches deftly the sources of Jenny's success. Jenny used gossip to play people against each other, she was always well-informed on every project and ensured that Richard relied on her for all information. Even the crude joke she sets up for the departing John seemed to underline her 'Don't mess with me!' image.

Fay found herself torn between, on the one hand, shock and despair and, on the other, an emotion which she did not name, resulting from the realization of her own hopes of promotion. She claims that she quickly became an insider to office intrigue (it became part of her 'own life') and also that she remained a fly on the wall. She seemed to despise an organization which treats people like Gill in such an offensive manner, yet she feels guilty about painting such a bleak picture of this company.

These mixed feelings are not unusual in organizations, when we find ourselves benefiting from the misfortunes of others or when we accept honours and rewards which sit uneasily with our misgivings and reservations. We face a dilemma: whether to become winners by playing the game by its not-too-pleasant rules, or whether to maintain our integrity by keeping outside the game – and so risk becoming 'losers'.

When one is surrounded by winners and losers, it is hard to remain detached – as our next story shows. Mirella, an Italian student, worked for a cosmetics multinational. She found herself an observer of a harsh game. Her story warns that even when people believe they are winners, they may in fact be losers in the 'meta game' – being played outside their field of vision.

Mirella's Story: Winners, Losers and Pawns

*I was really excited at the idea of working in a multinational in
Paris. My expectations were met on the very first day: working
conditions and facilities were all anyone could ever hope for. The
wealth of the company could be detected just by looking around
and observing: endless personal phone calls to unknown desti-
nations, free access to any type of office material (enough to set up
your own office at home!), drinks and snacks sitting outside each
office for the duration of the working day.*

*Who could possibly feel unhappy at the idea of getting up in the
morning to go to work in such a place? Yet, I soon found myself
wondering whether good working conditions and all sorts of
privileges attached to jobs actually outweigh the disadvantages of
joining the 'multinational mechanism'.*

*On 1 October, I joined a team of six people in the department
specializing in hairdressing products. I became assistant to Carol,
a charming Irish lady, and shared an office with Peter, of Swiss
origin, who had lived in Australia for the past twenty years. Three
months before my arrival he had been transferred with his family
to work at the company's headquarters, in Paris.*

*The atmosphere at work was so informal and friendly that I
soon became really close to Peter and Carol, my mentor. In less
than a week I was considered part of their team, and had access to
all sorts of informal discussions that were going on in the
organization.*

*Through Carol I learnt that Peter had found his move from
Australia very difficult; what was supposed to be a promotion had
turned out to be major upheaval. Life in Paris was far more
expensive than in Australia; his wife and daughters, born and
brought up in Australia, were struggling to learn French, his wife
unable to get a work permit in Europe. They were therefore stuck at
home without many opportunities of integrating into French
society. Still, Peter claimed that he was very happy to be in Paris, a
city he loved, happy to have made it to the headquarters, and
happy for his family to get to know France. He felt it would take
some time for them to settle down, but that things would get better.*

*Then, during one of our increasingly frequent chats, Carol
revealed to me that Peter would not stay at the headquarters in
Paris permanently, but would go and occupy a vacant position in
Germany. Paris was merely a stopover for him – but he did not
know that yet.*

For the organization, it did not really matter that he and his family were struggling to settle down in France. What really mattered to them was that Peter was the perfect man for the German job; his German was excellent and he would be able to carry out a job in Germany in the French way – which he was learning.

In the space of five minutes the destiny of a man I did not know that well, had been revealed to me. I felt I had become an accomplice in this 'multinational mechanism', where an invisible hand allocates resources in the most efficient way. I knew things about him that he would probably find out in about a year's time, by which time his family would have only just settled down. However, I could not warn him. My information came from the grapevine and was therefore not reliable. I was supposed to mind my own business and pretend I did not know. That was what everybody else was doing; this is how you were supposed to behave if you were working in that organization.

The fact that Carol was meant to be a close friend of Peter, implied that she should be the one to talk to him, I thought. I realized later that loyalty to the organization came first, even before friendship; nobody would ever dream of arguing against a decision made by the 'invisible hand'. Certainly, I thought, an offer to move to another country can be refused, but that is true only in theory. Once your destiny has been decided somewhere up in the hierarchy, the invisible hand will make sure you will find it too disadvantageous to refuse. In other words, the organization is willing to provide its employees with considerable privileges and good working conditions, but their identity is taken away from them in return. These are the rules, and once you are in the mechanism it is very difficult to get out; almost impossible.

The situation reminds me of those games where a child is supposed to fit an object of a particular shape into a hole of corresponding shape: the employees are just like the objects; there is a suitable hole for each one of them. The invisible hand, or rather, the decision makers that nobody ever sees or hears, are only concerned with finding the right holes for the right objects, because that is the solution of the game. Human values and circumstances are not even acknowledged to exist.

I still cringe at the idea of having one day a comfortable office in one of these organizations. Deep down, I will be conscious of the fact that I have become like a circle-shaped object and someone I don't even know is desperately trying to find the corresponding circle-shaped hole.

This story sounds a cautionary note – a man may be digging his own hole even as he imagines himself a winner. What seems like a triumph, a promotion to World Headquarters in Paris, may in fact be a temporary manoeuvre towards a less-lofty destination. If the previous two stories suggest that people are players in elaborate organizational games, sometimes winning, sometimes losing, this story suggests that individuals can also be pawns in other people's games. The fates of pawns have little to do with their own abilities and qualities; they are determined by the whims of players who operate in unseen arenas.

Mirella's vivid description of the opulence and wealth of the organization which impresses and seduces her, is not incidental to the story. The deal which the organization offers its employees is a share in its glamour and riches in exchange for a surrender of control and identity. This proves an unacceptable compromise, at least in Mirella's eyes. The company need not resort to anything quite so vulgar as threats; it can always make offers which people cannot refuse. Even pawns can be persuaded that they are true winners, especially if they cherish an ostentatious lifestyle and enjoy the resources which the organization lavishes on them.

Mirella makes no secret of her own embarrassment at knowing the destiny of a man, a destiny of which he is unaware. She feels an 'accomplice'. At one level this is absurd, since she clearly had no part in the machinations which determined Peter's fate. Yet, as she acknowledges, she feels complicity to a conspiracy of silence, a silence which is exacted by the organization as part of the deal. She offers two rationalizations why she did not tell Peter, someone she felt 'close to'. First, the information was not reliable, arising as it did from the grapevine; secondly, that if anyone should tell Peter, Carol should, since she was his friend. Carol's silence to Peter speaks volumes. In Mirella's mind, Carol has been seduced and compromised by the company. Thinking of her own future, the idea of being compromised by a comfortable office makes Mirella 'cringe'. Yet, her account suggests that this process may have started already.

The stories in this chapter reveal some of the less comfortable features of organizational experience. They also show how far removed from their daily experience many trainees find the rhetoric of teamwork, cooperation and togetherness; self-effacing team spirit makes only rare appearances.

Thinking On

1   Why does Geoff say that Paul is typical of the company as a whole? What, if any, evidence does he offer that Paul is not an isolated case of an arrogant executive?
2   Try to imagine Geoff five years after the story he describes. In what scenarios can you place him?
3   All three stories in this chapter involve grapevines. Reflect on what fuels the dissemination of information through the grapevine. How does the information change as it flows through grapevines?
4   Why do you think that Fay feels guilty about telling her story?
5   Have you ever found yourself in Mirella's situation, knowing something important about someone who was personally not aware of it? How did you feel? What did you do about it? How might you have reacted, had you been in Mirella's position?
6   Why do you think that Carol told Mirella, a junior employee, what she knew about Peter?

Reading On

Kapuscinski's (1983) description of Haile Selassie's court is perhaps one of the most compelling accounts of power games at grand political level, drawing its inspiration from Machiavelli's *The Prince*, an early classic of political theory. Vivid descriptions of organizational politics, winners and losers, have been offered by Kanter (1977, 1983). Kanter regards organizational 'politicking' as a normal and natural feature of all organizations, where many individual and group interests clash and where interpersonal, group and departmental conflicts may assume overt or covert forms. Her view of organizational politics is essentially pluralistic – a continuous process of alliances, conflicts and compromises between endlessly mutating interest groups and constantly negotiated rules of the game. In her view, women generally enter organizational politics at a disadvantage: in addition to discrimination and negative stereotypes, women find it more difficult to enter into supportive 'mentoring' relationships or alliances with powerful male figures without risking being compromised; they are also frequently excluded from informal forums, lobbies and networks where vital pieces of information may be collected.

Pfeffer (1981, 1992) and Kotter (1979, 1982) provide numerous examples of interpersonal rivalries and coalitions, within a broadly pluralistic framework. Lukes (1975) provides one of the most widely used typologies for analysing power in organizations. Willmott (1987) offers a strong critique of approaches (like Kotter's) which reduce organizational conflict and politics to interpersonal rivalries and disregard the underlying political-economic dimensions of managerial work. Along with other radical theorists (Beynon 1973; Burawoy 1979, 1985; Rosen 1985; etc.), Willmott views organizational conflict as a series of variations on an underlying theme, according to which capital seeks to control productive and administrative operations to maximize profit whereas workers seek to resist such controls. Even interpersonal or group conflict may serve the interests of capital, in as much as it keeps employees divided among themselves.

Morgan (1986) explores organizations as political systems and provides a comprehensive discussion of alternative approaches as well as of the sources of power in organizations. Charles Handy (1976) has provided a classification for comparing different manifestations of conflict – he distinguishes 'argument' (the discussion of differences), 'competition' (potentially fruitful contest, subject to rules) and 'conflict' (generally uncontained and disruptive). Radical theorists, on the other hand, scorn to distinguish between fruitful and disruptive conflict and prefer to classify conflict depending on whether it is overt or covert, individual or collective, institutionalized or unrestrained (Salaman 1981).

How do individuals respond to conflict? Thomas (1976, 1977) has argued that different individuals have different responses to conflict. He generates a two-dimensional matrix of assertiveness against cooperativeness; this leads him to postulate four extreme conflict orientations – avoidance, accommodation, competition and collaboration – and a moderate one, compromise. In spite of its appeal, such a classification appears to suggest that people have a consistent response to conflict.

Beynon, H. (1973). *Working for Ford*. London: Allen Lane.

Burawoy, M. (1979). *Manufacturing Consent*. Chicago, IL: University of Chicago Press.

Burawoy, M. (1985). *The Politics of Production*. London: Verso.

Handy, C.B. (1976). *Understanding Organizations*. Harmondsworth: Penguin.

Kanter, R.M. (1977). *Men and Women of the Corporation*. New York: Basic Books.

Kanter, R.M. (1983). *The Change Masters*. New York: Simon and Schuster.

Kapuscinski, R. (1983). *The Emperor*. London: Picador.

Kotter, J.P. (1979). *Power in Management*. New York: Amacon.

Kotter, J.P. (1982). *The General Managers*. New York: McGraw-Hill.

Lukes, S. (1975). *Power: A Radical View*. London: Macmillan.

Morgan, G. (1986). *Images of Organization*. Beverly Hills, CA: Sage.

Pfeffer, J. (1981). *Power in Organizations*. Marshfield, MA: Pitman.

Pfeffer, J. (1992). *Managing with Power*. Boston, MA: Harvard Business School Press.

Rosen, Michael (1985). 'The reproduction of hegemony: an analysis of bureaucratic control', *Research in Political Economy*, 8, 257–89.

Salaman, G. (1981). *Class and Corporation*. London: Fontana.

Thomas, K.W. (1976). 'Conflict and conflict management', in M.D. Dunette (ed.), *Handbook of Industrial and Organizational Psychology*. pp. 889–935. Chicago: Rand-McNally.

Thomas, K.W. (1977). 'Towards multidimensional values in teaching: the example of conflict behaviors', *Academy of Management Review*, 12, 484–90.

Wilmott, Hugh (1987). 'Studying managerial work: a critique and a proposal', *Journal of Management Science*, 24, 3, 249–70.

7

Compliance and Resistance

Why do we obey orders? This is a question which organizational theory has inherited from political philosophy. Machiavelli, writing in the sixteenth century, believed that people obey leaders out of either love or fear. He suggested that fear was the more solid foundation for a community where orders are to be obeyed. Some twentieth-century writers on organizations propose that neither fear nor love are as important as *calculation*. If you calculate that the benefits of following an order outweigh the costs of not obeying it, then you may comply with the order, feeling no particular emotion for the leader.

More recently, two additional ideas have entered this debate. First, that people may be obeying orders because they lack the ability to express their rejection ('she doesn't know *how* to say "no"'). Courage is part of this, but it also requires stripping layers of mystification which make one unable to imagine saying 'no'. Secondly, that people may be rebelling even as they appear to be conforming. Pupils who wear the regulation uniform may be conforming to the rules, but by leaving the top shirt button undone, they express their resistance to them. Compliance and resistance are not either/or responses. Orders may be obeyed willingly or unwillingly; they may, equally, be obeyed grudgingly, inaccurately, ritualistically or sarcastically. In all these cases, compliance and resistance can coexist in the same form of behaviour.

The three stories in this chapter indicate some of the subtle interplay between compliance and resistance. In the first story, Mark starts by relating the conflict between a personal commitment to be best man at a wedding and the demands of a working weekend, auditing for a prestigious firm of chartered accountants. He then details an intricate web of subtle pressures through which the company ensures compliance.

Mark's Story: How Svensons Turns us all into Willing Slaves

The incident occurred towards the end of my placement with Svensons, working on a high profile audit. The reporting deadline for this particular audit was renowned for being very tight, and our problems were further compounded by staff shortages (our team had been reduced from four to three) and the deadline itself had been moved up one week. This time pressure meant that I was expected to work more efficiently for longer hours – typically fifteen hours a day. I therefore decided it would be prudent to inform my audit senior in advance of a personal commitment I had on the audit's final weekend. I was to be the best man at a wedding.

During the three weeks of the work on this audit I found myself under increasing pressure to work longer hours. A common line used by the audit senior, with obvious undertones, was: 'I'm going to have to work later than usual tonight but you can go home now if you want'.

Things moved from bad to worse when a further colleague had to drop out unexpectedly at the end of the second week, with much of his work incomplete. It became increasingly obvious that I was going to be asked to work that final weekend, even though I had on numerous occasions subtly mentioned how much I looked forward to the wedding. After a subdued argument, I reluctantly agreed that it would be possible to work from early on Saturday morning until lunchtime, at which point I would have to go straight from the client to the train station.

On the Saturday morning I arrived particularly early to enable me to complete the areas I had to cover. By 10 a.m. I had virtually performed all my set tasks and was beginning to feel a sense of achievement and pride at being so close to finishing such a complex audit. At this point the senior turned and asked me:

'Have you finished that yet?'.
'Nearly, I just need about another hour. That should take me comfortably up to noon.'

I could tell what was coming . . .

'Could you do the royalty test?'
'I don't think I've really got the time.'
'Just do as much as you can.'

At twelve, having finished my prior work and touched on the royalty test, I mentioned that I would have to be going. 'Could you just finish the first section of the test in order to help me complete it later', said the senior.

In the end, I did not manage to get away until 1 p.m., feeling more a sense of relief than annoyance. Thankfully British Rail was not feeling its usual tardy self and I arrived only a few minutes late for the ceremony, to discover that the groom himself was also late!

Before my dealings with Svensons, I had come into contact with many other accountants through my work experience. As well as being useful experiences in themselves, I learnt a great deal about the attitudes held about the other firms. However else perceived, there was one common thread to all conceptions held about Svensons. This stereotype/reputation held that the company itself was 'a slave driver'; very tough in business, with workaholic employees. As is evident from my experiences, these analogies are not too far off target! It was a running joke with a friend on placement that I would phone him at home from work, sometimes as late as 10 p.m., and say 'I'm still at bloody work!'

Svensons are, however, firm believers in rewarding well and follow the only option really available to them – money. As I am the first to admit, this was a strong motivator, although I now feel not the only necessary one. The remuneration on offer was certainly able to satisfy my material needs. However, I soon discovered that they expected to 'own your body and soul'. This left little time for social recreation. Leading my own life became difficult and, at times, impossible – which itself led to monotony and frustration. However, the realization that I was able to 'jump from the train' in a matter of weeks was of great comfort.

My dealings with the senior on this job (and indeed any senior) were very non-confrontational. This behavioural trait was very unlike my normal outgoing personality, but was very much the result of my own competitiveness. The appraisal system within Svensons was stringent and revolved around a six-page form, completed for each audit by the senior. Well aware of this fact, and very determined to receive complimentary ratings, I deemed it beneficial to remain on an amicable footing with the senior. One of the tactics that I came across several times was for the seniors to ask if I wanted to go home before them. This, as they were well aware, had the opposite effect and made it more difficult to leave. From discussions with those colleagues who joined the firm at the same time as myself, it was obvious that I consistently worked more overtime than them. This leads me to the conclusion that the seniors I worked for were opportunists – they recognized that they could take advantage of me in this respect, and did!

Looking back on this short experience, I do now feel some pride – pride at doing more than just coping, but actually being an important and individual member of a highly-geared team that achieved its objective. This is, however, a considerable change from what I felt at the time: constrained, trapped. But then I did enjoy the buzz of excitement from that very same pressure.

We can start by asking whether Mark has complied or resisted. Clearly, Mark was forced to work on the weekend he had set aside for the wedding; he was forced to do tasks which were not 'his own'; he was forced to stay at work far too late for comfort; and he worked consistently far longer hours than stipulated in his contract.

His compliance is achieved through a variety of pressures, starting with the way the audit is presented as 'high profile' and 'renowned' for its tight schedule. Successfully completing the task is likely to bring status and recognition, rewards which Mark values. This is compounded by subtle attempts by his manager to induce guilt in him ('I'm going to have to work later than usual tonight but you can go home now if you want'). Mark assumes the mantle of martyrdom with a sense of humour ('At bloody work at 10 p.m.') and more than a trace of pride. The material rewards offered by the company are another source of pressure, seen by Mark as entitling the company to his 'body and soul'. Mark's own personality, seemingly susceptible to psychological pressures as well as to symbolic and material trappings, is perfectly suited to the organization.

His manager does not have to threaten; conflict never gets beyond a 'subdued argument'. The senior makes a series of escalating demands which Mark finds unable to resist. It is not so much the fear of a poor appraisal that leads Mark to give in, as his determination to receive a complimentary one. To that end, he seems prepared to put up with everything – everything, bar missing the wedding! And in order not to miss the wedding without engaging in confrontation (a quality he suppresses in himself), Mark has to deploy his own discreet tactics. Subtle hints, marking the time, arriving at work very early. The subdued argument is part of this process; it is a challenge which shows how serious Mark is about the wedding but does not significantly threaten his senior's authority.

The end, the wedding, is achieved, even if with difficulty. His senior, no doubt, would rather have kept Mark all afternoon, but he had to let him go. In this way, Mark can be seen to have successfully resisted the pressures to put work first at all cost, but he does so through a fair degree of, 'necessary', compliance.

In the next story, Tonya, a Norwegian trainee, tells us how she tolerates her subservient position as a member of the back office in a dealing room. Then, one day she has an outburst which breaks organizational taboos. Her resistance, unlike Mark's, is spontaneous and unpremeditated – its outcome uncertain.

Tonya's Story: The Day I Had Enough

My placement was in FinInter in London, a huge multinational which originates in the United States. The company is active in over 90 countries and prides itself on being the world's largest provider of corporate finance. I worked in the foreign exchange (FX) back office, where deals done by our 150 dealers were checked, payment instructions were added and queries addressed. My job was to resolve problems arising from deals. Much of the time, this meant going upstairs and talking to the dealers.

Now, you never told a dealer that he or she was wrong, even when handling those dealers who, throughout the whole of my placement, were never correct. You just briefly stated what the problem was and asked them to kindly look into it.

This particular incident involves Nick, one of the men who always 'cocked up'. This time he had mixed up the currencies on a deal. The payment was due in half an hour, so it was important to get him to amend the deal. I went up to see him, but Lee, also from the back office, was already talking to him about something else. Because my problem was urgent, I waited for Lee to finish. When Lee left, Nick glanced at me and then, to my surprise, left his desk and went over to another dealer, John, from whom we had heard juicy comments for quite a while. A group of dealers assembled and I could hear and see from their behaviour that they were not discussing business.

I went over and discovered that the reason for their behaviour was two pages from the Sun *newspaper filled with pictures of posing, naked women. Something inside me just snapped. I told Nick that my job was actually supposed to be a service to the dealers, to help make them aware of errors before they cost them money. I explained how much work I had to do and how much other dealers appreciated my corrections, so by ignoring me he was not only wasting my time, but his own colleagues' right to the service of the back-office officers. And with his error-statistics, I would imagine he had better things to do that to stare at 'page 3 girls'.*

I turned round, left my sheet of paper on his desk and departed.

My main emotion both then and now is anger. I felt I had been patient and taken much more stick and rude behaviour than was acceptable. The way Nick ignored me to go and look at page 3 girls was the straw that broke the camel's back. I also felt helpless and vulnerable. They were discussing naked women in detail in a room of almost only men, and I knew my views were in minority. I was afraid any reaction from me would be ridiculed. Writing about it now, I also feel proud for having had the courage to tell him off.

The Foreign Exchange dealers, nearly all men, were the most arrogant group of people I have ever come across in my life. If it had not been for me gradually understanding some of the reasons for their behaviour, an outburst like the one I have just described would have come much earlier. You need to appreciate the fact that the FX department is, at the moment, one of the best departments results-wise in FinInter, and this creates a feeling of invulnerability and extreme self-importance among those working there. I did not feel that this was a valid excuse for their behaviour; still, I learnt to accept it.

The back-office policy was to accept any amount of stick from the dealers, and then let it all come out afterwards when you were safely back at your desk. This policy was no good as it only helped to increase the hostility between dealers and back office. My telling the dealer off meant that I had broken the main taboo in the office. Over several weeks, I realized that this earned me much respect. I had done something many of my colleagues had wanted to do for years, but dared not to. The risk was smaller for me as I was only there for a short while. So, I achieved respect both from the back office and from some of the dealers. And perhaps, even more importantly, I respected myself more for having done what I felt was right.

Tonya's outburst is a minor classic of rebellion. A taboo of power has been broken and a voice has been found to express opposition. Mark, in the first story, resists through subtle hints and manipulation of his superior; Tonya resists, not by refusing to do something, but by giving Nick a 'piece of her mind', expressing her moral indignation at his behaviour.

Incidents like this are not very common in organizations, where people often endure in silence insults, harassment and innuendo. This is why when something unutterable finally gets said, its symbolic significance can be considerable. Power is reversed at a stroke. Tonya is not boasting in saying that what she did was what others had long wanted to do. She makes it quite clear that the back office was rife with anger and frustration at the dealers, yet not a word was ever said directly to them. Their centrality and self-importance offered them protection.

What brought about Tonya's outburst? As in the previous story, Tonya is irked by someone's cavalier attitude towards her position – an attitude such as 'she can wait; she's only back office'. Yet, it is the ostentatious leering which makes Tonya feel insecure and exposed. Helplessness and vulnerability turn into anger when compounded by insult.

It is the dealers' sexism – no less odious for being accepted as the prerogative of financial success – which Tonya finds unbearably insulting. When she speaks out, she crosses the boundary between acceptable behaviour (disparage and belittle dealers behind their backs) and unacceptable behaviour (tell them to their faces). What Tonya told Nick is perhaps less important than the act of crossing this boundary. It is interesting, however, that she reports a very controlled, calm, outburst. She did not rebuke his insulting behaviour but pointed out the urgency of her call on him. In this way, she held back from a head-on collision, which, she feels, would have laid her open to ridicule and disparagement. Instead her rebuke is thoroughly 'professional', giving him no leeway for retaliation.

Being able to speak freely, overcoming one's fear, is something which earns respect in organizations. It may be that other back-office staff started confronting the dealers, but is more likely that the incident is remembered as an isolated case of defiance and pride. What lessens the impact is that, in the eyes of her colleagues, Tonya did not have much to lose. Being 'a student' afforded her a certain immunity, while shows of defiance and pride by other back-office staff could have led to disciplinary action. Had Tonya been a permanent member of staff, her scuffle with Nick could have led to encounters during which Tonya may have been the loser. But for now, she emerges a clear winner.

The final story in this chapter is also one in which a woman confronts male power, albeit of a different sort. It is narrated by Jenny, who worked for one of Britain's largest car manufacturers. Here confrontation is the norm; displays of anger are routine. Unlike Tonya, Julie does not cross a frontier, but defends one against four angry shop stewards. She manages – just! Her account provides a insightful study of organizational politics, as well as an up-beat analysis of her personal reaction to a rugged environment.

Julie's Story: In the Thick of Organizational Politics

The incident which I believe best describes the company is a conversation, or rather an instance of verbal bullying, which occurred between myself and four shop stewards. I was as an Employee Relations Officer in the Assembly Plant. The shop stewards were all workers, but ones voted by their colleagues to represent the unions in the factory.

To put the conversation in perspective you have to understand that the atmosphere in the company was very aggressive, very confrontational. It is a them-and-us type attitude. There is a fine line between workers and management. On the surface it is often quite polite and very jovial. Underneath there are many class undercurrents and prejudices which make it all the more menacing.

The conversation itself was about a project I was dealing with where the foreman of the stores, a part of the factory where supplies are kept, required two more workers for his stores. He wanted two able-bodied men to be transferred from the main factory. Management, however, did not really want anyone to go to the stores, and if they did, would only allow so-called 'restricted' workers, i.e. those with physical disabilities.

The problem had been going on for a long time. Management had kept delaying a decision, and the union and stores foreman were getting very frustrated. When I arrived, it was the perfect opportunity for management to find a scapegoat, someone to take the heat. I was given the task of finding two suitable workers for the stores. Not an easy job! On one side, I had management who did not want able-bodied men going, and on the other I had the union who only wanted able-bodied men. Finding the right workers was taking some time and so I was put under pressure by both sides to find a solution.

Things were reaching boiling point. One morning I was sitting in my office and there was a knock on the door. In walked four very angry-looking shop stewards, shutting the door behind them. I was trapped in a small office looking up at these four men who were intent on catching their prey. Gone was the politeness, gone was the jovial manner. In its place was a scheming, cunning, aggressive – menacing even – attitude. Behind closed doors the real company emerges.

*The men wanted an answer from me, but they only wanted **their** answer. They wanted me to tell them what they wanted to hear, but I was not willing to do that.*

They worked together as a team. It was good to finally see true team spirit at the company! They would ask me a question and then, when I replied, they would come back with: 'Oh, so this is what you mean' or 'Are you saying this?'

It took all my concentration and quick thinking to stay ahead of them and ensure I said the correct thing. It is very easy to become nervous and start to babble, and then you say what they want to hear. They would constantly try to twist my words.

The conversation consisted of them asking me questions, me trying to answer, and them twisting my answer. They would take it in turns to ask questions and would alternate quickly, trying to confuse me.

I managed to defend myself and didn't say what they wanted me to. After a few more minutes I had enough and just made an excuse about a meeting. I asked them to leave. They did not leave in a jovial manner; the old facade was not quite back in place. I had frustrated their attempts to ensnare me in their web of words, and in so doing I had passed my first initiation test to life at the company. Not a pretty picture.

At the time, the incident was very unnerving. I was not at all prepared for it. I had been aware of the undercurrents but I was not prepared for the naked aggression and the total mistrust which were revealed during this event. Trust seems to be the key. The shop stewards did not trust my motives or my actions. Being the naïve student that I was, I had actually been trying to please everyone – and not just the management. But the shop stewards could not see this. My first lesson, therefore, was: try as you may, you cannot please everyone and so please those who pay your salary or write your appraisal. The hard truth is that they are the only people who count. This statement is a far cry from the student who began her placement at the company.

When I started at the company I was actually expecting the worst. I had heard many stories and had been warned by everyone about life at the company. Unfortunately, the company lived up to my expectations. It is a place where deals and bargains are struck in the corridor outside meetings. It is a place where verbal fencing is a legitimate weapon to use in a continuous game of chess, where the goal is to out outmanoeuvre your opponent. This may all sound a bit melodramatic, but it is the way I perceived working for the company. It was all a game and, believe me, I learnt to play very quickly.

From reading this it may sound as if I hated every moment of my placement. On the contrary, I loved it! Conversations like the one I have just described were scary at first, but they also got the adrenalin rushing. Working under constant pressure in a fast moving environment is fun. It can be stressful but I found I could cope, and that built up my confidence. The verbal battles were exhilarating. They certainly get the mind working.

Life at the company taught me a great deal. I believe it was the best placement I could have had. Unfortunately it makes most other jobs seem tame to me. Looking back I can see how it built my confidence and my determination. I learnt how to stay calm and see the funny side of crises. The only way to survive at the company is to stay calm. I also learnt an important lesson in fitting-in. After my initial shock at seeing the mask slip I understood more the need for a facade. You cannot work in an atmosphere of naked aggression. The jovial exterior was to make a working relationship possible. I no longer felt it was being two-faced to be nice one minute and to fight the next. By mutual agreement, we all played our parts within the factory.

Julie's story takes us to a world apart from the discreet and tactical game at the chartered accountants' firm, or the silent discontent of the bank. Here confrontation is head-on, face to face, and involves implied as well as physical intimidation.

One is immediately struck by the fact that Julie was entrusted with the key role in such an explosive issue. She suspects that management deliberately framed her in this role, intending to use her as a scapegoat in order to accede to the shop stewards' demands. She also indicates that the shop stewards believe that they can now get the desired concession from management, by exploiting a young trainee's inexperience and timidity. And indeed, Julie starts by believing that there are always solutions which can please both sides. But she soon shifts ground, realizing that this is not a game in which everyone can be a winner. She is determined to hold her own and resist the verbal bullying.

Her description of the 'conversation' between her and the stewards is a brilliant account of politics, where words become weapons, and with each side trying to outmanoeuvre the other through subterfuge, confusion and deception. Those who can use words effectively, who can invoke precedents, who can point out contradictions in the arguments of others, who can confuse and outwit, or verbally intimidate their opponents, enjoy a considerable strategic advantage over their adversaries. These factors can allow the weaker position to prevail over the stronger one. Julie observes that had she panicked and allowed any contradiction, uncertainty or ambiguity to creep into her words, the stewards would have easily overcome her resistance. Under pressure, she might, perhaps, have made a 'small' concession, hoping that she would resist the full demand; yet Julie realized that this was an all-or-nothing issue. She also recognized that keeping one's wits in verbal jousting was as important as holding one's ground. She succeeded on both counts.

It is instructive that at no point in her story does Julie discuss the relative merits, moral or practical, of the two positions being argued. She is caught up in the exhilaration of the battle – carried along by the 'adrenalin' rush. Is it sensible, or right, that physically disabled men should carry loads? One suspects that once she starts asking such questions her resolve may be undermined. This is characteristic of the confrontational atmosphere prevailing in the company. It makes questions like 'Could my adversary possibly be right?' totally unthinkable. Julie has fast taken an uncompromising position, reflecting the tough culture of the organization. The 'hard truth' she claims to have learned is that only those who paid her salary 'counted'.

In order to survive, Julie must forget about goals and values and concentrate her mind on the means, the arguments, the tactics. The purpose of the game is not questioned, it is only the winning strategy that concerns her. Any ethical context is 'defined out' of the situation. This is a salutary comment on organizational morality. Yet Julie's single-mindedness commands respect in the organization, possibly even from the shop stewards who were the losers in that confrontation.

The three stories in this chapter are different instances of organizational resistance. They are snapshots from a continual political process. Each of the trainees reports an instance where by wit and subterfuge, courage and defiance, they scored significant victories in the course of this process. Pride is the predominant emotional quality of all three stories. Such emotional responses serve as a reminder that power and organizational politics can be a tonic for those nearer the bottom of the organizational hierarchy, as well for those at the top.

Thinking On

1 Make a list of different ways in which people can express resistance in organizations. Then try to classify expressions of resistance according to three or four criteria which seem important to you.

2   What is the difference between rebellion and resistance? What are the different ways in which managers in organizations can deal with rebelliousness or resistance of subordinates?

3   It is sometimes argued that the powerful can rely on brute strength to get their own way in organizations. How can the less-strong members prevail in organizational power games?

4   Is losing your temper a good or a bad thing? Think of the last time you witnessed an emotional outburst, like the one described by Tonya. What brought it about? What were its consequences? What determines the effect of seeing someone lose their temper?

5   Aggression frequently goes unnoticed in organizations. Discuss the ramifications of the different forms of aggression evidenced in the three stories of this chapter.

Reading On

Many of the concepts and readings suggested in the previous chapter also apply to this one. Weber's (1948) classic formulation of power juxtaposes legitimate authority to non-legitimate violence or coercion. Authority implies that subordinates recognize the superior's right to give orders. Weber envisaged three sources of legitimate authority: charisma (the extraordinary qualities of the leader), tradition (the sanctity of long-standing custom) and a rational system of rules. The first two are based on emotion, the last on calculation.

A large part of Michel Foucault's work is aimed at illustrating that power operates in more subtle ways than Weber envisaged. People may be obeying regulations or acting in particular ways as workers, patients, administrators or as gendered male and female sexual beings without being conscious of obeying orders, willingly or unwillingly. (See Foucault 1965, 1971, 1976, 1977; Burrell 1988.) Knights and Vurdubakis (1994) have offered an interesting reading of Foucault's conception of power which also entails within it the concept of resistance. Martin (1990) has shown how language, notably the language used by male senior executives, systematically and invisibly disadvantages women, by incorporating covert assumptions of a discriminatory nature.

More traditional Marxist and post-Marxist scholars have been sceptical about Foucault formulations which, they feel, underestimate the conscious, motivated resistance of willing subjects when confronted with oppression. Beynon (1973) has provided one of the most lasting descriptions of industrial confrontation and worker resistance in his study of Ford. He highlights the elaborate games that go on between management and the work-force and various tactics of subordinates' resistance to the power of their superiors. Forms of employee resistance, including sabo-tage, absenteeism, pilfering, output restriction, as well as direct confrontation like strikes and work-to-rules, have been studied by numerous authors including Edwards (1979), Thompson (1990), Collinson (1994), Knights (1990) and Willmott (1990).

Resistance to sexist oppression, ranging from negative stereo-typing and discrimination to bullying and sexual harassment, has been discussed by many of the contributors to the collection by Hearn et al. (1989), and by Austrin (1994) and Wilson (1995).

Symbolic forms of resistance have been explored by Rosen (1984, 1985) and Gabriel (1991, 1995). These authors combine psychological and sociological insights to explore individual and collective resistance which does not so much challenge the power of those in control as undermine its claim to legitimacy. Jokes, humour, embellished stories, gossip, fantasies and disfigurement of symbols may be used to this effect.

A type of organizational resistance that has recently attracted the attention of researchers is whistleblowing: the exposure by organizational insiders of corruption, abuses of power or decep-tion of the public (Jackall 1988; Sims et al. 1993; Rothschild and Miethe 1994).

Austrin, Terry (1994). 'Positioning resistance and resisting position: human resource management and the politics of appraisal and grievance hearings', in J. Jermier, W. Nord and D. Knights (eds), *Resistance and Power in Organizations*. pp. 25–68. London: Routledge.

Beynon, H. (1973). *Working for Ford*. London: Allen Lane.

Burrell, G. (1988). 'Modernism, post modernism and organizational analysis 2: the contribution of Michel Foucault', *Organization Studies*, 9, 2, 221–35.

Collinson, D.L. (1994). 'Strategies of resistance: power, knowledge and subjec-tivity in the workplace', in J. Jermier, W. Nord, and D. Knights (eds), *Resistance and Power in Organizations*. London: Routledge.

Edwards, R. (1979). *Contested Terrain: The Transformation of the Workplace in the Twentieth Century*. London: Heinemann.

Foucault, M. (1965). *Madness and Civilization*. New York: Random House.

Foucault, M. (1971). *The Birth of the Clinic*. London: Tavistock.

Foucault, M. (1976). *The History of Sexuality*. Harmondsworth: Penguin.

Foucault, M. (1977). *Discipline and Punish*. London: Allen and Unwin.

Gabriel, Y. (1991). 'On organizational stories and myths: why it is easier to slay a dragon than to kill a myth', *International Sociology*, 6, 4, 427–42.

Gabriel, Y. (1995). 'The unmanaged organization: stories, fantasies, subjectivity', *Organization Studies*, 16, 3, 477–501.

Hearn, J., Sheppard, D.L., Tancred-Sheriff, P. and Burrell, G. (eds) (1989). *The Sexuality of Organization*. London: Sage.

Jackall, R. (1988). *Moral Mazes: The World of Corporate Managers*. Oxford: Oxford University Press.

Knights, D. (1990). 'Subjectivity, power and the labour process', in D. Knights and H. Willmott (eds), *Labour Process Theory*. Basingstoke: Macmillan.

Knights, D. and Vurdubakis, T. (1994). 'Foucault, power, resistance and all that', in J. Jermier, W. Nord and D. Knights (eds), *Resistance and Power in Organizations*. pp. 167–98. London: Routledge.

Martin, J. (1990). 'Deconstructing organizational taboos: the suppression of gender conflict in organizations', *Organization Science*, 1, 4, 339–59.

Rosen, M. (1984). 'Myth and reproduction: the conceptualization of management theory, method and practice', *Journal of Management*, 21, 3, 303–22.

Rosen, M. (1985). 'Breakfast at Spiro's: dramaturgy and dominance', *Journal of Management*, 11, 2, 31–48.

Rothschild, J. and Miethe, T.D. (1994). 'Whistleblowing as resistance in modern work organizations: the politics of revealing organizational deception and abuse', in J. Jermier, W. Nord and D. Knights (eds), *Resistance and Power in Organizations*. pp. 252–73. London: Routledge.

Sims, D., Fineman, S. and Gabriel, Y. (1993). *Organizing and Organizations: An Introduction*. London: Sage.

Thompson, P. (1990). 'Crawling from the wreckage: the labour process and the politics of production', in D. Knights and H. Willmott (eds), *Labour Process Theory*. London: Macmillan.

Weber, M. (1948). *From Max Weber: Essays in Sociology*, ed. H.H. Gerth and C. Wright Mills. London: Routledge.

Willmott, H. (1990). 'Subjectivity and the dialectics of praxis: opening up the core of labour process analysis', in D. Knights and H. Willmott (eds), *Labour Process Theory*. Basingstoke: Macmillan.

Wilson, F.M. (1995). *Organizational Behaviour and Gender*. London: McGraw-Hill.

8

Games

Winning and losing are fairly unambiguous experiences in most organizations. What is more unclear is the nature of the games being played. As customers or clients of organizations, we rarely get a glimpse of the games played behind the scenes. When we do, it can come as something of shock, especially if the smooth exterior hides chaos and strife – like the fraught kitchen of a smart restaurant. But even when we are actually working behind the scenes, we may find yet more metaphorical curtains, behind which different games are being played from the ones we witness directly.

Here we enter the realm of multiple realities. Which is the 'real' game and where is it being played? Which is the stage where the 'big game' is being conducted and where is it? The answer is that many different games are being played simultaneously in organizations in a variety of arenas. What is more, players are often trying to define the rules to suit their own interests. Some of the most important games involve determining the rules according to which other games will be conducted. How should a position be filled (rather than 'who should fill it')? Should a unanimous decision be required on an important issue, or is a majority decision enough? Should the same formula be applied for resolving a budget dispute as was applied last year?

Most of our students were not prepared for the complexity and multitude of organizational games they encountered. Some were surprised, even shocked, when they happened upon practices which they did not know were there, or that did not seem altogether right or clear – but which certainly affected their work. It was particularly revealing when 'information' and 'facts' turned out to be highly charged politically, twisted and turned to suit the interests of different groups.

In the first two stories, presented together here, we get a picture of organizations with one major backstage curtain, behind which there are executives calling the shots, regardless of what work the students do. Both of these stories take place in marketing departments – Brenda's in a shipping company and Thor's in a major tobacco corporation.

Brenda's Story: Massaging the Statistics

'Transea has a duty to provide shipping services throughout the world . . . having due regard to efficiency, economy and safety of operation.'

The above quote from the Transea annual report sums up the company's professed goals. During my placement as a Marketing Assistant with Transea's Marketing Department, my job was to compile statistics on the customers' needs and priorities; I soon realized that reality did not always square with such grand objectives, as is shown by a conversation, which epitomized my impression of the organization. It was an informal conversation between myself and a senior manager, to whom I presented the results of a piece of research on which I had spent a lot of time. He looked at the results and his sole comment was: 'Can't we massage the statistics?'

I first thought that the manager wanted to 'massage the statistics' in order to use them as evidence supporting his professional judgement. My view now is that this was not the case. Knowing something of the man, I'm sure that personal ambitions dominated his concerns – prestige, career advancement, salary and an easy working life. He chose to work with people who were hand-picked as 'yes men', and then controlled their promotion prospects according to their cooperativeness. Massaging the statistics was routine within the department, even though it made a mockery of conducting research work. It also indicates the manager's lack of professional respect for his analysts. He expected them to dilute their objectivity for his personal, egotistical interests.

The dubious business ethics demonstrated by this manager were not, in my experience, shared by all of his subordinates. For instance, the research work that I undertook was supervised by an analyst who displayed the utmost integrity in his work and never compromised his professionalism. I would therefore suggest that the pursuit of different objectives by some of Transea's managers was one source of the internal managerial conflict that was rife in the organization. Massaging the statistics was one manifestation of this conflict, showing that many decisions are primarily governed by personal motives rather than meeting the organization's goals.

Thor's Story: Smoke-screen

While working in the market research department of Slocum and Driver Tobacco Corporation, I came to learn, from several conversations with other employees in the department, that much of the work they did was merely confirming decisions already made by top management. Yet the function of the department was supposedly to advise them on what decisions to take.

For over two weeks I was given the task of analysing Holden, our flagship brand and one of the world's best selling cigarettes, which had been losing its share of an already declining cigarette market. All relevant data showed that the reason why Holden had been under-performing was not that Holden smokers were quitting or switching to other brands (in fact, loyalty rates among Holden smokers were significantly higher than those of other brands), but that no new smokers were attracted to Holden. The reason for this was that the general image of Holden was that of an unhealthy, harsh-tasting cigarette smoked largely 'by people in ghettos'.

These conclusions had already been drawn by others before me, yet top management insisted on asking why so many Holden smokers were quitting. This obviously led to duplication of work and a certain amount of frustration for those who believed that the wrong decisions were being made in an effort to turn the brand around. My boss would often laugh at some of the requests sent down from 'upstairs', and would comment, in not so many words, that top management, especially the chairman, were out of touch with reality, old-fashioned and in a world of their own. Perhaps top management knew something we did not, in which case they should have informed us; their policy decisions seemed to make a mockery of the market intelligence we had.

Forecasts for the next month's sales, which determined how many cigarettes were shipped out of the factory to the distributors, were not based on realistic assumptions but adjusted to meet management's objectives for the end of year sales. This became a comedy as the young woman who was making the forecasts had to alter them several times in succession before they were accepted. Our entire work seemed to be to say what top management wanted to hear. Yet, there was not any real resentment towards top management. Most middle management were using the company as a stepping-stone to start up their own companies or to move to better jobs, since the higher echelons of the company were reserved for the time being.

Brenda and Thor both found the results of their own work, or the work of their department, redefined. It was as if the stage they were operating on had its backcloth lifted to reveal new, and powerful, players who would tell them that black had to be made to look white. So, accurate statistics had to be altered to fit the games played by these players – games which made little sense to those below them.

Brenda was clearly affronted by such behaviour and took a moral stand. It seemed to her utterly unprofessional and hypocritical to 'massage the statistics' to fit the personal and political predilections of managers. Coming straight from a university, where precision and objectivity are dominant values, she was shocked to discover that 'research' has a far different meaning in a marketing department in an organization from the one it has among academics. 'Truth' may be an absolute value in academic research, but in the marketing department the 'truth' is flexible and there are many different ways of stretching it to suit particular interests. Undesirable truths can be neutralized or disguised, their sources can be discredited, their implications can be misrepresented. 'Being economical with the truth' – an expression coined by a senior British civil servant to imply that he may not have 'told the whole truth, but did not lie' – is a common ploy in the attempt to redefine a game to one's advantage.

Subordinates often possess information which can crucially influence the games being played way above their heads. For example, giving information which displeases or embarrasses one's superior can be risky. Throughout history, many of the bearers of bad news have found themselves on the receiving end of harsh justice – so it may be easier to tailor the message to suit what the powerful want to hear, as Thor described so well. Being a junior employee, he could not understand why Slocum and Driver's top management kept asking the same research question – yet seemed uninterested in the precise answer. Perhaps they did not like the racial overtones of the market research findings and were searching for a less emotive reason for its lack of appeal to a wider market. Or maybe they were looking for a scapegoat, inside or outside the organization, to blame for the brand's poor performance. Really, Thor was in no position to understand what game was being played.

Being part of a game, the rules of which are unclear, can be frustrating – as Brenda's and Thor's stories illustrate. After all, it is their work that is compromised, distorted or ignored. It is harder still if they suspect (as does Brenda) that, far from serving the wider interests of the organization, the game is driven by someone's personal ambition.

The next story also reveals uncertainty about the source of the game being played. What sets it apart from the earlier two is that the narrator, Arne, is an active participant in the game. Also, the game turns out to be rather nastier than the one he thought was being played. And, finally, he encounters several other games unfolding simultaneously.

Arne's Story: The Alien

Two weeks before the start of my placement at Chatfields Bank, a new director was appointed to run the Finance and Taxation Department of the Eastern European Group (EEG). I will refer to him as the 'alien'.

The alien was a strict accountant, and quite senior in the Chatfields' hierarchy. For the first couple of weeks I was too 'fresh' to understand much of what was going on around me, but after a while I started to familiarize myself with the department. The working atmosphere gradually became tense, and there was a lot of 'talk' in the department – the alien was the target.

It all came to a head early one morning at the beginning of August. In the office there were five people: the alien, two 'bankers', a graduate and me. Just before eight o'clock the alien was called up by the head of EEG, who wanted to see him. It was extraordinarily quiet in the room as he left, and not a word was said when he returned five minutes later. The alien went over to his desk, and removed all his papers from the drawers. I remember watching him as he stacked the files, and put them into his briefcase. He cleared the top of his desk, grabbed his overcoat and umbrella, and quickly exchanged words with one of the 'bankers'. Without looking at me or any of the others he walked out of the room; the silence was complete until we heard the doors on the lift shut. We never saw the alien again.

The next couple of hours felt strange. It was like being in a classroom with kids and no teacher. Just after nine o'clock, when everyone had arrived, the whole department went up to see the head of EEG. We were told, in very simple terms, that there would be no talk of the incident; 'as far as we were concerned the alien had resigned'. Not a lot was said during the next couple of hours, but there was a general feeling of relief and a renewed working spirit. The incident culminated when the whole department went down to the pub at lunchtime – more as a recuperation than a celebration. At the same time I did not feel like celebrating; it was as if all the gossip and talk previous to the sacking made me feel guilty.

The incident is to me more than just an ordinary sacking; it's a story of cultural collisions and interpersonal rivalry which led to an intolerable situation in the workplace. I would also like to emphasize, before I continue the discussion, that the sacking was a result of a deliberate strategy by certain people in the department to get rid of the alien.

It is important to note that EEG Finance and Accounting was a 'strong culture' department. Everyone knew their place, and within a relatively liberal working environment everyone did what was expected of them. The alien did not understand the culture and, in addition, he came from a department where people behaved by 'the book'.

So how did I see this? What concrete examples show us that the alien did not fit in? One of the first changes in the office, which in some peoples' eyes may be trivial, was a formal rule (presented to the staff in a memo) demanding that all documents produced in the department should have the initials and the date in the bottom left corner. Nothing unreasonable in that, one would have thought, but for the staff it was an unreasonable and bureaucratic rule which did not make sense in their culture based on **trust***. The alien continued with such small changes, without sensing that he was on a collision course with the 'EEG culture'.*

The incident told me that in a company there is a hidden network of people who have immense power, mainly through gossip, malicious talk and knowing the right people. The alien was sacked as a direct result of this, and even though I was happy to see him go, I will never feel comfortable about the way in which it happened.

Arne and his colleagues were rather like people witnessing the twitching body after a hanging. They were transfixed at the dramatic spectacle of the 'alien's' departure; a mixture of awe and delight. Although Arne was happy to see the unfortunate director go, he felt that the man had received rough justice. Arne's ambivalence was sharpened by the guilt he felt from personally bad-mouthing the director.

How do we explain the new director's demise in terms of the games being played within the department? In one corner, behind one curtain, the hand of the Head of Department is plain to see.

After all, he dismissed the man. But Arne talks elliptically of 'a deliberate strategy by certain people to get rid of the alien'. There are veiled hints that Arne himself has been part of a conspiracy of colleagues to unseat the director, and he is now trying to distance himself from it. Perhaps he did not seriously anticipate the end happening quite so suddenly and brutally; clearly, he was not aware of the size of the stakes in the game – a person's career and livelihood.

In another quiet corner we can envisage conspirators of rather more senior rank than Arne, supporting each other's dislike for the director. Soon this shapes into a small 'movement', a behind-the-scenes whispering campaign to rid themselves of him. Whispering campaigns can be effective, yet their outcomes are unpredictable. Some of the people who enjoyed a good laugh at the expense of the alien may not have meant to end his career with the company; others may have intended to do precisely that. The Head wields the axe, but it is placed in his hands by the victim's own immediate staff. The guilt Arne feels has to be contained, so he takes pains to find evidence that the director was a cultural misfit; the very nickname, 'alien', seems to make his demise less harsh. Yet, the evidence presented by Arne is hardly earth-shattering. The visit to the pub sums it all up – a drink after a funeral.

Can we still talk of 'games' when people's lives and careers are at stake? Looking at organizational life as a series of games is not intended as a trivialization of the consequences or the interests at stake. Games can be fun, but also very serious. They can have uncertain consequences and dramatic conclusions. Viewing organizational politics as one huge game is compelling, because it highlights the passion that goes into winning and the pain of losing. It also underscores the idea that there are rules which shape proceedings.

An organization, however, is infinitely more complex than a board game, a game of cards or a sports event. In none of the stories discussed in this chapter are we ever clear about the precise nature of the game being played. What we get are some clear images of episodes in the games: the massaging of the statistics, the wilful disregard of research findings, a sacking. Our students' view of organizational games is like that of a spectator who has only a partial view of a pitch on which several different games are going on at once, with different rules but interconnected stakes and outcomes. This can be challenging but also confusing, especially when the spectators discover that, unknowingly, they too have become players in the game.

Thinking On

1 What games have you observed in an organization that you have belonged to? Can you distinguish between healthy games and destructive ones?
2 Have you, or someone you know, discovered that you were a pawn in someone else's game? Describe the circumstances and feelings.
3 Do you think that Brenda and Thor were unrealistic in getting disturbed by witnessing the systematic twisting of information?
4 What game did Arne think was going on, before he discovered that the alien's future had been at stake?
5 Look at Arne's story from the perspective of the sacked director. Put yourself in this man's shoes and construct a story from his point of view.
6 Is it sensible to talk about organizational games, when people's careers and livelihoods may be destroyed as a result?

Reading On

The use of game theory in analysing political conflict (Myerson 1991), economics (Friedman 1990; Kreps 1990) and business (Gardner 1995) has become increasingly common. Game theory is the systematic study of games and was founded in the middle of the twentieth century by John von Neumann. Game theory examines different types of games, different game strategies, risk, information, cooperation and competition, as well as the psychology of the game-player.

The psychology of winning is pre-eminent in Jennings' (1971) and Maccoby's (1976) vivid portrayals of executive games. Radford (1986) has explored the explanatory power of game theory when applied to organizational decision making, while Sims et al. (1993) describe different types of games and game outcomes. They examine, for example, how a zero-sum game in which only one party wins may be transformed into a game in which several parties win simultaneously.

Morgan (1986) has analysed the strengths and limitations of different metaphors for describing organizations, including that of games. Mangham (1986) prefers a dramaturgical to a games metaphor of organizational action (organizations as theatre), but makes an effective use of exchange theory to observe how different political actors within an organization seek to define games to their own political advantage.

One of the most trenchant critiques of games permeating every aspect of social life, including life in organizations, is offered by Lasch (1980) who views them as a manifestation of a shallow and self-obsessed culture of narcissism. Lasch argues that the gradual spilling of a games mentality into every aspect of social life devalues both social life and sport itself. Sport is degraded because it becomes trivialized, reduced to an ephemeral pursuit of hype and sensation.

The final story in this chapter raises the issue of unemployment and the effect of sackings, both on the person being sacked and on his or her colleagues. Studies by Kaufman (1982) and Fineman (1983) reveal that the sacking and redundancy of professional employees can be personally devastating. Such people can lose important parts of their self-identities, which can be hard to recover.

Fineman, S. (1983). *White Collar Unemployment*. Chichester: Wiley.

Friedman, James W. (1990). *Game Theory and its Applications to Economics*. Oxford: Oxford University Press.

Gardner, Roy (1995). *Games for Business and Economics*. New York: Wiley.

Jennings, E.E. (1971). *Routes to the Executive Suite*. New York: McGraw-Hill.

Kaufman, H. (1982). *Professionals in Search of Work*. New York: Wiley.

Kreps, David M. (1990). *A Course in Microeconomics Theory*. Princeton, NJ: Princeton University Press.

Lasch, C. (1980). *The Culture of Narcissism*. London: Abacus.

Maccoby, M. (1976). *The Gamesman: New Corporate Leaders*. New York: Simon and Schuster.

Mangham, I.L. (1986). *Power and performance in organizations*. Oxford: Blackwell.

Morgan, G. (1986). *Images of Organization*. Beverly Hills, CA: Sage.

Myerson, Roger B. (1991). *Game Theory: Analysis of Conflict*. Cambridge, MA.: Harvard University Press.

Radford, K.J. (1986). *Strategic and Tactical Decisions*. Toronto, Ont.: Holt McTavish.

Sims, D., Fineman, S. and Gabriel, Y. (1993). *Organizing and Organizations: An Introduction*. London: Sage.

9

Who gets the Blame?

Mistakes are human. What makes them intriguing is the unpredictable relation between a mistake and its effects. A tiny lapse may lead to considerable human, physical and financial costs. Conversely, major blunders may sometimes amount to trivial losses or even unexpected benefits. Numerous types of organizational story are spawned by mistakes. Mistakes can be amusing, especially when committed by pompous individuals who receive a well-deserved comeuppance; they can be tragic if they result in unnecessary suffering and pain. Elsewhere, mistakes can be read as symptomatic of deeper organizational stresses and quandaries, failures in 'the system', or internal conflict and demoralization.

One of our first thoughts when hearing of an error is 'Who is to blame?' If we happen to be involved, we often quickly think of many reasons why we are *not* to blame, or of excuses for why it happened. In both cases we may be trying to shift responsibility onto someone or something else. Alternatively, we may find ourselves being held responsible for mishaps over which we had no control, feeling scapegoated or framed.

These are the themes of the stories in this chapter told by new organizational recruits. They tell of small or large organizational injustices – and the anger which results from this kind of victimization.

Kevin's story is first. It is drawn from his experience in British Plastics, one of Britain's largest manufacturing companies. It illustrates how much bitterness can be generated by a seemingly trivial incident.

Kevin's Story: The Missing Icon

The majority of the staff of seven in my office were a little bewildered by the two new PCs which arrived that morning. It was especially puzzling for the two supervisors, who were both computer illiterate.

After a couple of hours 'fiddling with her machine', Mandy Whitehill, one of the supervisors, decided to go home an hour early (4 p.m.). As I needed to use WordPerfect I used her PC, and after about half an hour I completed my task, and returned to my desk and mainframe to work, **not having touched the Lotus package** *(which was also installed on her machine).*

The next morning, Mandy started to use her new machine, and was obviously in a state of confusion; after about an hour, she asked myself and Richard, a colleague, to help out. The problem was that her Lotus icon (the Lotus sign on the computer screen, necessary for entering the Lotus software) had disappeared from her screen. As Richard was much more familiar with the new machine, I returned to my desk to continue work on other tasks. Richard, however, was unable to regain the icon and the company's computer specialists were sent for.

As they struggled to correct the problem a mini 'investigation' started, to find who had altered the configuration of the new computer. As time passed, I began to realize that Mandy was quietly blaming me, after she was informed that I had used her machine the previous evening. She made some sarcastic remarks, in effect accusing me of making the mistake: 'This wouldn't have happened if someone hadn't messed around with my machine last night'.

I protested my innocence – stating that I hadn't used Lotus, but I was subconsciously found guilty by the office and, henceforth, I didn't use Mandy's machine again as a matter of principle. This caused a great deal of friction between Mandy and myself, because it was obviously she who had made the mistake, and it riled me to be a scapegoat for someone who didn't have the strength of character to admit her own mistakes.

In my opinion I gained a great deal of knowledge from this incident. Not only was Mandy exercising her formal power but also taking advantage of our relative positions within the hierarchy of our office to influence the opinions of the other office members; the more I protested my innocence, the further I fell into a grave which had been dug for me.

Group cohesiveness within my office was non-existent. How can Mandy have expected me to be cohesive with her, and the other members of the group, after they had just showed an obvious lack of trust, and a willingness to accuse a member of the office who is far from guilty?

Another factor I noticed, that was inconsistent with British Plastics's public image and reality, was that delivery-deadlines to customers were constantly being abused and broken. The staff attitude to this within my office was 'tough luck, it's not our fault'. Whereas the image which British Plastics likes to, and does, communicate is that they are a very efficient and caring company – **not very true***! This is especially so in Mandy's case, as she was continually criticizing students, and in my opinion her attitudes got the better of her.*

The internal company propaganda was a farce, compared to what was actually happening within the offices. There is a system within the company which enables dissatisfied staff to air their grievances, hailed by the monthly circular as one of the best innovations in their Industrial Relations Department for some time. I complained I had been unjustly accused. My complaint didn't succeed; it was met with quite a cold response. I left with awful feelings of **frustration, angriness** *[sic],* **uselessness,** *and* **betrayal.**

What we find interesting in this story (and many similar ones) is the amount of anger generated by a relatively 'minor' incident. As his story unfolds, we can feel Kevin getting progressively angrier, eventually expressing fury and despair. The incident becomes an emblem of all that was unjust about the organization and its management; Kevin's anger, hostility and bitterness seem to condense down and focus on this event. It is noticeable that his distress is somewhat out of proportion to his injury – to judge by his story, he was not disciplined, merely admonished. His punishment was moral, not material.

Why then did Kevin feel so outraged about being blamed for a routine computer mix-up? It is difficult to know whether the incident is the cause of Kevin's hostility towards his manager and British Plastics, or whether his hostility coloured his interpretation of the incident. We hear, for example, that Mandy 'continually criticized students', something which may have caused friction even before the event with the computer. What makes the incident important is that it goes beyond 'office politics', illustrating the moral indignation which many of us experience when we feel unjustly accused.

Anger is not so much the result of exploitation or harsh treatment, as of injured pride. Not only is Kevin's pride injured, but all the usual protestations of innocence only help to reinforce his guilt – in the eyes of others in the office. No amount of talking could get him out of the 'grave' that Mandy had dug for him. As a trainee, he was seen as an outsider, his word carrying little weight. Additionally, messing up other people's computers appears to be precisely the type of behaviour that negative student stereotypes thrive upon. Kevin thus becomes Mandy's perfect scapegoat in the office. His outrage reflects the fact that he feels totally trapped.

Moreover, Kevin contrasts his own victimization with the ease with which (in his eyes) everyone else in the office escapes responsibility, constantly breaking promises to customers with a simple 'tough luck, it's not our fault'. This suggests something about the nature of responsibility in organizations – while a minor mishap may be oppressively pinned onto someone with hardly any evidence, a major blunder may be readily concealed.

This theme of justice and injustice continues in the next story. Christoph, a German trainee, worked for a major transnational photographic corporation, in their market research department. The company was based in Stuttgart.

Christoph's Story: 'Oh Dear! £50,000 Down the Tube? Let's Pretend it Never Happened!'

It was a normal day at work. I was sitting at Dr von der Schulenburg's desk, after having had the usual 45 minute coffee break; we were discussing the merits of various types of market research. Herr Doctor von der Schulenburg is about 60 years old and came to the market research department of IMAGO about 15 years ago, after having worked for a market research institute. In short, one can say that he is a very intelligent man, slowly turning a bit senile.

During our conversation he pulled out the study he had to present the following week. It was based on a major survey comparing our films to those of our competitors. The interviewees were shown a card with a photograph from an IMAGO film, and a similar one from one of our competitors, and were asked to choose which one they would buy. Beneath the photograph, in small print, were the technical specifications, and in large digits the set price for the film. Our competitors' films were kept at one price level (DM5.95) but the price of the IMAGO film varied from card to card (DM4.95 to DM9.95). IMAGO had put two of their films into this interview, one was the Superchrome and the other was the higher quality IMAGO Ultra.

When Dr von der Schulenburg showed me the results he pointed out that he could not figure out why almost nobody chose to buy the higher quality Ultra film, even when it was offered at a lower price. I decided to take a closer look. I soon found the mistake. Every film was supposed to have 36 exposures, but the Ultra film only had 12 exposures written on the pack. When I showed this to Dr von der Schulenburg, his eyes just widened and he said: 'Oh Scheiße, I must have given the photographer the wrong film pack! I'll just make sure then that I don't mention the Ultra results in my presentation next week'. I had to promise not to tell anyone what had happened – something that gained me some respect.

Half of the results of the survey were rendered useless and nobody really cared about it. The study cost IMAGO about one-to-two weeks of preparation time by Dr von der Schulenburg, and then approximately £50,000 for the interviews, conducted by a market research institute. Yet, it seems that as long as nobody knew what went wrong, you can sit down and fiddle a bit with the results, and everything continues as if nothing had happened. This is the track the whole company seems to run on. Everyone just has his little job to do; when something goes wrong, it's usually not noticed at all or it is noticed when it's too late. If someone looked at the survey a few weeks later, he might decide to scrap the Ultra film from production, although, in reality, it might be quite profitable.

When I came to IMAGO I wasn't too sure if I would like to work in a large company, since I had always worked in small, fast and highly-productive companies before. Besides, the study of bureaucracy in my first year at university didn't really make me look forward to being a part of one. This incident underlined my fears. I believe that only a few people in this company work to their full potential. From a friend, I found out that the employees in the sales department liked to indulge in a game of cards after their coffee break. Maybe things are different for those who managed to climb the ladder to a respectable position. I say this because I hardly ever saw my boss. He always seemed to be off to some important meetings.

Whenever I had sat down with Dr von der Schulenburg before this incident, I was always quite happy and flattered by the way I was treated. He, and others, were very willing to teach me something about market research. After this incident, though, I found my respect for the whole company, and especially for Dr von der Schulenburg, slowly diminishing. I didn't ask Dr von der Schulenburg as many questions any more.

I now know that I don't want to work in a large company when I leave university. I had more fun working in various photo shops

*during previous summers, where there was more of a challenge to
the work, more decisions to make and more people to meet.*

In contrast to Kevin's story, which centres upon the unfair
blaming of an innocent person over a small issue, Christoph's
account focuses on a rather major blunder which gets white-
washed and goes unnoticed and unpunished. In Kevin's story we
get the impression that hardly anything goes wrong in a
bureaucracy without someone being blamed for it; for Christoph,
no one seems to notice or care. Responsibility becomes so diffused
and unfocused that no one shoulders the blame. Christoph
wonders whether higher up in hierarchies things may be different, but his experience at IMAGO appears to confirm his worse
fears.

People were worried about being found out when things went
wrong, so they hid their errors. Christoph became an uncomfortable accomplice to this culture. Should the blunder ever come to
the surface, his 'promise' not to tell anyone placed him in a
compromising position. This was somewhat offset by the extra
respect he gained from colluding with Dr von der Schulenburg;
yet, at the same time, his own regard for the Doctor and for the
organization declined.

Christoph's account does not make it totally clear, but it seems
that it is the cover-up, rather the mistake, that accounts for this.
It is dishonesty and fear of admitting an error, rather than
incompetence, that troubles him. Dr von der Schulenburg, in
spite of his age, authority and title, has acted essentially like a
schoolboy who has kicked a ball through a window and worries
about being found out. The organization, for its part, seemed to
encourage the classic bureaucratic attitude of timidity – 'cover
your backside' – and lacked mechanisms for ensuring that
blunders of this nature were not repeated.

Christoph found himself colluding with his superior to conceal
an error. In the following story, Basheer is encouraged by his boss
to 'blame the system' when he discovers a mistake. The incident
took place in a firm of metal brokers.

Basheer's Story: 'You Haven't Made a Mistake!'

*One day we had tremendous problems finishing off the computing
of the dollar position. Eventually I found the error and it was
embarrassing to learn that it was my fault. Shamefully I went to*

see my manager to explain why the process had been delayed, and that I was the one to blame.

*'Listen,' he started, '**You** haven't made a mistake, but **the system** has. Whenever something is wrong you must come and tell me that the accounts system has screwed up. The system will lose prestige and value, whereas you have gained recognition because you spotted the error. You see, this company likes winners.'*

There are two different types of learning stages when you join this sort of company. You initially face a formal, tedious description of the company, but then the real learning begins. This happens through a long, informal process, where you gain knowledge from experience through certain incidents, like the one above. These teach you how to adapt to the environment in which you are working. BTMC is well-known as a sound, conservative commodity broker and it actually lived up to that expectation. But when I added all the 'bits and pieces' of my experience together, I discovered its invisible power structure. You are not a winner by admitting your mistakes!

It is hard to overestimate the impact that an incident like this can have on people getting their first taste of organizations. 'Adapting to the environment in which you are working' can quickly become a euphemism for absorbing all the 'political necessities' of survival, such as lying, deception and subterfuge, coupled with the moral excuses for doing so. Basheer felt embarrassed and ashamed of his mistake, yet at the moment when he felt vulnerable, his boss gave him a way out of his difficulty – never blame yourself, blame the system.

It can be argued that blaming 'the system' is a very healthy response when mistakes are made. It certainly obviates the need for a human scapegoat and depersonalizes blame. Instead of orienting the organization's efforts to censuring a single person, it looks at the organization's processes and seeks changes which will prevent similar mistakes happening again. In this way, 'blaming the system' can become a first step towards organizational learning and improvement. Yet, more commonly, blaming the system is the classic excuse for avoiding change and responsibility. It is a failure to recognize and examine a mistake, and therefore a failure to learn from it.

Cynicism, dependence and petty-mindedness rapidly set in when a young recruit is told by superiors never to acknowledge his or her mistakes. Yet, not all dealings with errors and failure end in cynicism and blame-shifting. The final story of this chapter combines several themes raised by earlier stories: bureaucratic inertia, personnel being out of touch and self-deception. But, significantly, it shows that if a superior can accept responsibility and criticism, both the trainee and the organization may emerge from an unpleasant experience as winners. The story is told by Isabelle. She worked for a multinational food company which markets several world-famous brands. The firm is keen on graduate recruits, taking on several hundred each year.

Isabelle's Story: Whizza Pizza or Damp Squib?

'So what do you know about Farmright?' I was asked at my interview. My thoughts flashed back to all of the posters that I'd noticed on my way to the interview room. 'Well', I said, 'it consists of Gleam chocolate, RX snacks, Whizza pizza, Fruity drinks and many other famous brand labels.'

That was the beginning. My placement was in the Graduate Recruitment Department, assisting with the run-up to, and eventually, the 'milk-round' itself (where employers tour universities, making presentations to final year students, hoping to cream off the brightest graduates). One incident that has stayed in my mind took place during the company's Autumn term presentations.

Having been privileged to attend Farmright's recruitment presentation at Birmingham University, I felt that I was in the position to view the evening from two perspectives. First, as someone representing Farmright Int. and, secondly, as a student who will, no doubt, be attending something similar during my final year. However, because I am also still a student, I think that those who attended the presentations felt they could be honest and criticize the presentation. In fact, many students commented that the presentation was bland, appeared extremely 'dated' and was not dynamic enough. This view may have been highlighted because many of them had recently attended a very high-powered business game, run by one of our competitors, which they had found exciting and stimulating. By the end of the evening I concluded that approximately half of the students to whom I had spoken had expressed a negative view of the presentation.

During our evening meal the director, my boss and all three presenters, constantly praised the entire presentation. They commented how 'keen' the students were. I sat there thinking, 'Were these the same students that I spoke to?' In the light of their agreement with each other, I thought it more appropriate to keep my personal opinion about what the students thought to myself.

In the days that followed, my boss and I discussed very briefly how the event went. I did mention the fact that some of the students who spoke to me had given me negative comments, but I did not feel it appropriate to judge their views as being the norm. The Birmingham presentation was mentioned no further.

But it was. A month later at a Marketing Recruitment Seminar, the Personnel Director approached my boss asking who was responsible for the Birmingham presentation, and what had gone wrong. My boss was bewildered. Apparently, a student who had attended the presentation had commented on how awful the evening had been – it was, in her words, 'the worst presentation I had attended'. My boss, who was by now beginning to worry somewhat, phoned me to ask again for my views about the presentation. My views suddenly became valued. Hence my next project was to generate feedback from students about individual presentations (via questionnaires) and collate it, concluding with some suggestions about changes/improvements that should be made. The structure of the presentations had not changed in the last four years, but following my report a new type of presentation and a new front cover for the graduate brochure were 'in the pipeline'.

When my placement commenced, I regarded Farmright as simply a very successful company. Ask me now, and I still think that it is a very successful business; however, Farmright Head-quarters need to take a closer look at the image they portray to future employees. From my experience, I found that it takes outsiders to inform Farmright of changes that should be made – otherwise, the company is unwilling to recognize that any prob-lems exist.

Isabelle's account shows how strong the pressures not to rock the boat can be. Twice she notes that she did not think it 'appropriate' to relate the negative comments which she had heard. Criticism is always difficult to accept, and can be especially difficult to give in an organization where one does not want to fall out with one's seniors. Under these circumstances, work groups, departments or even entire organizations can deceive themselves with myths about their own 'excellence', 'quality' and 'performance'. Isabelle perceptively comments that it often takes an outsider, with little to lose, to start the process of dismantling some of these delusions.

In her story, the outside influence is a strong, though casual, complaint which reaches a senior manager of the organization. At this point, many organizations might have reacted defensively, for example, by saying 'Untypical!' or 'Had an axe to grind!' or 'We don't want recruits like this!' Isabelle's boss might have sought to blame those directly responsible for the presentation – or even Isabelle herself for inviting the 'wrong' type of student to the presentation.

Instead Isabelle's boss, admittedly feeling somewhat exposed, took the criticism seriously. Isabelle's views which may have been irksome or inappropriate earlier, suddenly became highly respected and were used as the basis for improving the company's package to prospective employees. It is telling, then, that Isabelle did not share the sense of disillusionment of the students in the previous three accounts; she maintained her high opinion of the company.

The stories in this chapter show how much both organizations and individuals can lose by failing to acknowledge their mistakes and learn from them. They also demonstrate the importance of justice and fairness, if people are not to withdraw and take up highly defensive positions – covering their own backs, avoiding victimization, scapegoating others. Yet, the strong emotions voiced by the students show just how difficult it can be to attain such ends.

Organizational hierarchies become highways along which blame travels: superiors blame subordinates for filling in the wrong forms or pulling the wrong levers; subordinates blame superiors for designing forms and levers wrongly or giving the wrong instructions. Apportioning blame can become a highly unpredictable business. Under these circumstances, people may learn the simple, but demoralizing, lesson that the best approach is simply to protect themselves.

Thinking On

1 Why do we experience so much outrage when we feel unjustly accused of something? What drives our moral indignation? Do we respond similarly in work and non-work settings?
2 Are you sure that Kevin is telling the truth? Is there a chance that he did mess up Mandy's computer, knowingly or unknowingly?
3 What do you think is the role of computers in Kevin's story?

Could the story have focused on some other piece of office machinery? Why does he consider it necessary to inform us that Mandy was computer-illiterate?

4   What do you think that Dr von der Schulenburg should have done in order *not* to lose Christoph's respect? What would have been the right thing to do upon discovering his costly blunder?

5   'I was only obeying orders' is a common excuse, equally for crimes as for mistakes. When should a superior carry the responsibility for his or her subordinate's behaviour, and when should the subordinate carry the responsibility?

6   Guilt, shame and embarrassment feature prominently in the stories in this chapter. What are the differences between them?

Reading On

Mistakes and errors have not attracted quite the amount of academic research they merit. Freud's (1901) pioneering work suggested that 'Freudian slips' fulfil some unconscious desires, such as for self-punishment, to be noticed or a desire to break something. Freudian slips in organizations may represent the venting of unconscious hostility against one's employer, a form of involuntary sabotage of the organization. More recently, researchers like Broadbent et al. (1982), Reason and Mycielska (1982) and Reason (1990) have taken a cognitive approach in order to identify different types of errors (e.g. recognition, repetition, omission, etc.), and they have studied personal and environmental factors which affect error-proneness. Wehner and Stadler (1994) provide a gestalt theory of human errors which combines some psychoanalytic and cognitive insights.

Blaming, victimization and scapegoating, on the other hand, have received considerable attention (Hirschhorn 1988; Baum 1987). When wrongly accused, individuals frequently feel threats of annihilation out of proportion to the actual blame placed on them. The reason for this may be that such accusations trigger memories of early childhood experiences which were perceived as life-threatening. The strong feelings of rage, anxiety and fear generated by such events may be explained by the phenomenon of regression to an earlier, more vulnerable age.

Errors, of course, may be experienced equally as opportunities for personal or organizational learning. Morita (1987), the founder of Sony, gives a perceptive account of the impossibility of learning without recognizing mistakes (1987, 150 and *passim*). McCall et al. (1988) provide numerous examples of managers discussing and learning from their own mistakes. There is an underlying tension in literature between the potentially cata-strophic effects of simple mistakes and the need to make mistakes in order to learn from them (Kotter 1995).

Particular disasters, like those striking Chernobyl, the space shuttle Challenger and the Piper Alpha oil rig, have attracted considerable attention (Schwartz 1989, 1990; Pattecornel 1993). In addition to cognitive lapses and technical and organizational shortcomings, self-deception and resistance to criticism have been discussed as contributing causes to such disasters (see Kets de Vries and Miller 1984; Schwartz 1990; and Gabriel 1992).

The stories in this chapter also raise questions of morality in organizational life. Grand moral principles of right or wrong are soon redefined according to the pragmatics of survival, blaming someone else or the 'system'. Sims et al. (1993) devote a chapter of their textbook to this phenomenon, explaining how it can result in huge organizational frauds. Jackall (1988) has usefully elabor-ated the concept of 'moral rules in use' to describe how organiz-ational norms subvert moral behaviour, a perspective related to Argyris and Schön's (1974) contention that 'theories in use' rather than peoples' declared 'theories in action' determine how people actually behave. Fineman (1996) has further developed this thesis in terms of 'enacted moralities' to show how managers take actions which end up damaging the natural environment.

Argyris, C. and Schön, D.A. (1974). *Theory in Practice: Increasing Professional Effectiveness*. San Francisco, CA: Jossey-Bass.

Baum, H.S. (1987). *The Invisible Bureaucracy*. Oxford: Oxford University Press.

Broadbent, D.E., Cooper, P., FitzGerald, P. and Parkes, K.R. (1982). 'The cognitive failures questionnaire and its correlates', *British Journal of Clinical Psychology*, 21, 1–16.

Fineman, S. (1996). 'Constructing the green manager', *British Journal of Management*, (in press).

Freud, S. (1901). *The Psychopathology of Everyday Life* (Standard Edn), Vol. 6. London: Hogarth.

Gabriel, Y. (1992). 'Putting the organization on the analyst's couch', *European Journal of Management*, 10, 3, 348–52.

Hirschhorn, L. (1988). *The Workplace Within*. Cambridge, MA: MIT Press.

Jackall, R. (1988). *Moral Mazes*. New York: Oxford University Press.

Kets de Vries, M.F.R. and Miller, D. (1984). *The Neurotic Organization*. San Francisco, CA: Jossey-Bass.

Kotter, J.P. (1995). 'Leading change: why transformation efforts fail', *Harvard Business Review*, 73, 2, 59–67.

McCall, M.W., Lombardon, M.M. and Morrison, A.M. (1988). *The Lessons of Experience*. Lexington, MA: Lexington Books.

Morita, A. (1987). *Made in Japan*. London: Fontana.

Pattecornell, M.E. (1993). 'Learning from the Piper Alpha accident: a postmortem analysis of technical and organizational factors', *Risk Analysis*, 13, 2, 215–32.

Reason, J. (1990). *Human Error*. Cambridge: Cambridge University Press.

Reason, J. and Mycielska. K. (1982). *Absent-Minded? The Psychology of Mental Lapses and Everyday Errors*. London: Prentice Hall.

Schwartz, H.S. (1989). 'Organizational disaster and organizational decay: the case of the National Aeronautics and Space Administration', *Industrial Crisis Quarterly*, 3, 319–34.

Schwartz, H.S. (1990). *Narcissistic Process and Corporate Decay*. New York: New York University Press.

Sims, D., Fineman, S. and Gabriel, Y. (1993). *Organizing and Organizations: An Introduction*. London: Sage.

Wehner, T. and Stadler, M. (1994). 'The cognitive organization of human errors: a Gestalt theory perspective', *Applied Psychology*, 43, 4, 565–84.

10

Networks and Empires

There is no end to the fascination generated by secret societies, like the Freemasons, drug cartels or spy networks. Such outfits provide material for journalistic exposés, as well as for rumour, paranoia and, above all, conspiracy theories. 'Straight' organizations, on the other hand, as reported in the financial pages of newspapers or through advertisements of products, have a far less intriguing image – at least to outsiders. To many insiders, however, every organization has its own secret society or societies, where important decisions are taken. In this chapter we will explore stories which focus on two important ingredients of the secret organization – networks and empires.

Networks are loose formations which cut across organizations. We hear of a group of people referred to as 'the Oxbridge brigade', or 'the boys from x', where x can be any of a small number of prestigious public schools, or cliques composed of people with similar ethnic or religious backgrounds. The implication is that people who belong to these networks are joined by a superior, often invisible, bond. Network members will systematically assist each other to the detriment of those outside the network.

The existence of such networks is very difficult to confirm or deny. Often, the very fact that a handful of people from the same school, the same ethnic background or the same sexual or political orientation happen to work in the same organization is taken as evidence of the existence of a network. This 'fact' is then taken as demonstrating that the network functions to disadvantage those who are not its members. Conspiracy theories, where people imagine themselves disadvantaged by scheming networks, can then easily germinate with little need for any practical proof. But proof is extremely difficult to obtain, since secrecy is of the essence to these networks.

Not all networks operate to disadvantage others, nor do they all operate covertly. Universities, for example, spend much money developing networks of alumni. Such networks offer their members a sense of continuity and of belonging to a community of people with whom they share a common heritage. Older members can offer their experience, money and wisdom to younger members or to the network as a whole, while enjoying the prestige and honour that their contribution generates. On the other hand, networks which systematically exclude others from positions of influence can become pernicious for organizations, cultivating indulgence, arrogance and decay.

Networks are sometimes the basis for empire-building. Some organizations resemble a constellation of fiefdoms, fiercely contesting territory and seeking to score tactical victories at the expense of their competitors. By appointing individuals who they can trust on the basis of their social, ethnic or educational backgrounds, the 'barons' running these fiefdoms seek to ensure loyalty to themselves and a strengthening of their own position within the organization.

In the first story, George finds himself unwittingly a member of a network he did not know existed. The benefits which he derives from it seem to overwhelm him. He gives a rich account of the dramatic effect networks can have on an individual's life.

George's Story: Old Boys

Is there really such a thing as an old boys' network? As an ex-pupil of a private school I had seen little evidence of it and had substantial doubts about its existence. I put it down to feelings of jealousy amongst people who had not managed to achieve their ambitions.

However, my placement has served as an example of the way it can work. I would not suggest that this is typical, but what I did and where I worked for the most part was to hinge on such connections.

My initial posting had been to an old and declining factory in Merseyside. It belonged to KMK, a pharmaceuticals multinational. I found myself with little work to do; indeed, my presence there appeared to generate considerable resistance. Factory staff seemed to see my arrival as something of an invasion of their territory and a reflection that they weren't doing their work properly. After signalling my problems to my company supervisor I was promised an interview with someone from Group Development at the company's Head Office in Brussels.

I went to this meeting a little nervously – the first time I had come face to face with a director of a multinational company. However, my fears were proved misplaced. James Fairclough's opening salvo, after glancing at my CV, was, 'So, you're a King's boy are you? I was at Repton – used to play cricket against you. Do you know so-and-so?'

The meeting became less of an interview and more of a trip down memory lane for him, accompanied by the occasional 'Yes' or 'No' from myself as I hadn't much idea of what he was talking about – he had some thirty years on me. The interview finished with a promise that he would 'see I was alright'.

The following Monday I got a 'phone call from him asking whether I had a current passport (yes) and whether I could fly out on Thursday (yes). Basically he had 'seconded' me onto an executive commuter package with its accompanying flights back and forth every weekend, a room in a four-star hotel and unlimited meal expenses.

As far as the work went, he again took me under his wings, and although I was expected to put in considerable hours (14 hour days more often than not), he made sure that any problems I encoun-tered along the way were ironed out.

I have to admit that I did take full advantage of this position and (I hope this is confidential) ran up expenses of around £25,000 over my six months. At one time this included an apartment on the Champs-Élysées in Paris.

However, this was not the only benefit of networks. In both Brussels and Paris there is a very tight-knit expatriate com-munity. This was to be very important to me. From thinking I would be alone in a country where I did not know anyone or even speak the language, I found myself being welcomed with open arms by everybody out there. The introductions from my mentor led to some very strong friendships. It is an atmosphere I love, and though everyone works extremely hard, there is a strong com-munity spirit and sense of fun. Very few went back to their families in the evenings, so they relied on each other for support.

To be honest though, I do feel a little guilty about the fact that I was out there while there were individuals with whom I had worked in the UK, eminently better qualified than myself, but who could not find a senior position in the company. One case in point was a girl in Merseyside, who had graduated a year previously. She was doing project-work across the country, while trying to find a permanent position in the company. She could have benefited far more from a project at Head Office, and would have been of more use to the company than myself. I found it very difficult to look her in the eye after I came off that initial telephone call during which I received the invitation to take the job.

In summary, I look back on this experience and realize that I
have been extremely fortunate and privileged. I realize that I did
not get there on my own merits alone, but I don't think they were
disappointed with the work I did there. I have been invited back
for further projects, not only by my boss out there, but by others
with whom I worked. I do feel that this is a more honest
judgement of my capability. No matter which school I had been
to, I don't think that I would have been invited back if I had been
nothing but a liability to their department.

It is worth noting how far-reaching the consequences of meeting
James Fairclough turned out to be for George. His humdrum
placement in the company's backwater in Merseyside was transformed overnight into a taste of corporate jet-setting, and his
travels in Brussels and Paris introduced him to an expatriate
network which may shape his future life and career. In years to
come, George may come to regard his meeting with the old boy
from Repton as a truly providential moment in his life. George's
account of his interview with Fairclough is a classic – a trip
down memory lane, with the occasional nod on his part.

Looking back at his colleagues in Merseyside makes him feel
guilty; he is the lucky one who has escaped from mediocrity, not
through courage but through a combination of family circumstances and luck. George shows self-awareness in not attribu-
ting his elevation to, say, his intelligence or charming
personality, but to lucky coincidence. This, of course, does not
preclude the possibility that Fairclough genuinely formed a high
opinion of George, seeing him as the sort of young man he once
was, and who would be a credit to the company.

It is probable that Fairclough would deny that his support for
George owed anything to the public school connection. Alternatively, he may well argue that, by giving George a taste of the
higher echelons of the organization, he is promoting someone
with a 'background' he can trust. George, for his part, has
already started to employ a classic rationalization for his good
fortune. His connection may have opened the door for him, but
it was through merit that he managed to advance beyond
that. The very fact that the door opened for him somewhat
undeservedly, raises his obligation to prove himself worthy of
Fairclough's favour. This is a common defence of networks –
hiring or promoting someone like yourself (from the same club,
religion or family) means hiring someone who will not let you or
the network down; someone who will be grateful to you and will

seek to prove him or herself worthy of the privileged treatment received.

The two stories which follow give further, but contrasting, pictures of the operation of networks. The first, told by Manish, focuses on the sad fate of an individual who gets caught up in departmental wrangling in the Civil Service: in many government departments empires operate discreetly, and their competition is slow, tactical and deliberate. The second story, Richard's, tells of an instance of almost open warfare between departments.

Manish's Story: The Firing of Helen

My placement was spent in the Manpower Planning Section, a part of the Operational Research Division of a large government department in Whitehall. The Civil Service has a reputation for being highly bureaucratic. It has been criticized for having too many levels in its hierarchy, which are seen as preventing it from performing efficiently. My department, in particular, also suffers from a reputation of being disorganized and unprofessional. This is consistent with what I observed during the period I worked there. Disorganization and lack of professionalism were more often than not the outcome of machinations through which different groups in the department tried to gain an advantage over other groups. Perhaps the most notable incident I witnessed was the dismissal of Helen, a secretary.

Helen was Dr Mayhew's secretary. Dr Mayhew was the head of the division in which I was employed. Helen was not a direct employee of the department, but she had been working as a 'permanent temp' for several months. She was regarded as highly competent and efficient by our division. However, other divisions saw her as bossy and arrogant. They claimed that she often overstepped the mark by intruding into other people's responsibilities. A colleague from another division told me, 'She thinks she's God! She thinks she runs this place'. Helen's direct line manager was Rosemary, a member of the Central Support Unit, who was in charge of all the secretaries working for the divisional heads. To put it mildly, Rosemary and Helen did not get on, having had several heated conversations in public.

In June, Dr Mayhew went on holiday leaving Helen to supervise a complete reorganization of his files, assisted by Mr Harris, another member of Rosemary's Central Support Unit. Mr Harris kept receiving visitors whilst working in Dr Mayhew's office. Helen decided that, as Dr Mayhew's office contained 'official documents', no visitors were to be allowed into his office. Mr Harris complained to Rosemary who was furious. Rosemary accused Helen of having no authority to ban people from Dr Mayhew's office. Helen believed that she had been acting in the best interests of Dr Mayhew and the organization. After several very heated arguments Rosemary dismissed Helen. Rosemary then left on holiday.

Dr Mayhew returned from holiday to find himself without a secretary and his files in a mess. He immediately reinstated Helen. However, when Rosemary returned from her holiday, she discovered that Helen had been reinstated without her approval. Rosemary argued that she was the only person with the authority to 'hire and fire' secretarial staff who worked for divisional heads; she then said that Helen had not had the necessary educational qualifications for the job, and therefore could not be employed by the department, which insisted on minimum requirements being observed. Dr Mayhew argued that he, not Rosemary, was effectively in charge of Helen, since he assigned work to her, he filled in her appraisal form and he could judge how well she was suited for the job. After a lot of squabbling, Dr Mayhew conceded and Helen was finally dismissed.

This all shows how difficult it is for individuals to understand how they fit into a complex structure, what is expected of them, or who is their real master. Throughout my placement, I personally experienced the same problem. No one took the time or trouble to explain what my exact role was, what my responsibilities were, or what I was supposed to be doing. Perhaps Helen had a similar problem. Being unaware of exactly what her job and her role in the organization were, she unwittingly strayed into other people's territory and paid the penalty for it.

The incident shows how arbitrarily the rules and regulations were applied. Helen should never normally have been considered for the job, because she did not have the qualifications. However, she proved to everyone in the Division that she could do it extremely effectively. Again, in stopping visitors from using Dr Mayhew's office while he was away, Helen was following the rules, though she was probably not the person with the authority to enforce them. Yet, her dismissal shows that the rules in the department were only used as a smoke-screen for departmental

*politics, whenever it suited a particular power group or network.
As a fellow trainee commented, 'I wouldn't work for the Civil
Service when I graduate. Too many layers, too many cliques. Not
the place for me.'*

Going on holiday is a dangerous business in the highly politicized
atmosphere described by Manish. While her champion is away,
Helen is fired by a member of a different fiefdom, who takes the
opportunity of scoring a tactical victory in organizational politics.
Rosemary then finds that, in her absence, Helen has been
reinstated.

The field has been set for a confrontation over who is boss – Dr
Mayhew or Rosemary. In this confrontation, the rules of the
organization are alternately disregarded or applied with exaggerated emphasis – on the letter rather than the spirit. Manish
does not explain why Dr Mayhew conceded – was he placated with
some compromise offering, or did he lose outright? This will make
little difference to Helen, and seems irrelevant to Manish himself,
who clearly does not enjoy the prospect of being the next victim of
departmental machinations.

Why did Helen become a person over whom an important
skirmish was fought? Her loyalty to Dr Mayhew, her willingness
to 'overstep the mark' and venture onto other people's turf, her
assertiveness and unwillingness to shy away from confrontation
– all these features made her a suitable target for hostility from
other departments. They also made her an ally of Dr Mayhew,
who could not be seen to abandon her. A battle, therefore, had to
be fought.

It is interesting that, while Helen was dismissed in the first
instance for exceeding her authority, her final dismissal was on a
technicality – that she, apparently, lacked the 'formal qualifications' required for the job. Now, seeing as it was Rosemary
herself who had appointed Helen (she was 'the only person with
the authority to "hire and fire"'), it was her responsibility to check
Helen's qualifications. Appointing someone without the necessary qualifications is rarely a problem in highly politicized
cultures, where individuals are employed as much for their
loyalty and personal 'fit', as for their specialized expertise. Yet,
when Rosemary discovered that Helen's loyalty was with Dr
Mayhew, not with her, she had no qualms in invoking her lack of
qualifications to secure Helen's dismissal.

In the our final story, Richard describes the break-up of an 'empire' in a large international bank. This is no mere skirmish or tactical posturing, but major warfare. The result is not the loss of one person's job, but those of several hundred employees.

Richard's Story: Atlantic-Pacific Empires

Atlantic-Pacific is one of the major banks within the UK; it has recently become part of one of the largest banking groups in the world outside Japan. I'd like to talk about the empires within Atlantic-Pacific, with particular reference to the breaking up of one of them – Wholesale Operations, a group of fifteen departments under the control of one person.

Atlantic-Pacific has a very organic organizational structure. Many jobs appear to have developed around the managers, rather than managers around jobs. Some managers have more than one department under their control. Certain people within Atlantic-Pacific have managed to take control of many disparate departments; these I classify as empires. The organizational structure of Atlantic-Pacific is a mishmash of empires. A common phrase used by the employees to describe many of the managers was 'empire builders', people who literally try and accumulate as much power as possible.

The incident which best highlights my theory of empires was the splitting-up of a major empire, following the early retirement of the Head of Wholesale Operations. According to the grapevine (Atlantic-Pacific is rife with rumours and gossip), he had been forced to retire by an alliance of other empires. No one was to replace him, instead the fifteen departments which made up Wholesale were carved up and divided between the other empires. The week after I left, my own department was split: one half merging with its equivalent department in Central Operations and the rest going to an empire called BIBS.

At the time that the breakup was announced I actually thought it was quite exciting. A massive management decision had been made. It was dynamic; it meant business. This was the glamorous, action-filled, side of banking. As my understanding of the true reasons behind the breakup of Wholesale increased, my opinions changed. Most people have heard about office politics and the 'power game', but when you witness it at close range for the first time, as I did, it is quite a shock. I personally believe a few of the top empire builders became concerned about a forthcoming restructuring of the company. They decided to strengthen their positions by riding the storm of change, at the expense of another empire. It might be a natural pattern to defend what is yours, but it still appears rather callous to me, even if, as my boss, the head of Wholesale claimed, he will be given an excellent retirement package.

The response of staff to the breakup, and the resulting redundancies, was rather off-hand. They seemed almost indifferent to the political wrangling going on around them. I suppose they were used to hearing about redundancies. I had quite frequently heard people say 'they have sent the axeman in' and 'have you heard about so and so, he has gone to the block'. Such jokes were told with relief that the axe had not fallen on them. Following the breakup, many people I had known and dealt with in my job were made redundant. There was one particular day in my department when no one did any work at all. They all sat there waiting to be called to a meeting and individually told what their future would be. What I failed to realize fully at the time was the extent to which their livelihoods depended on their jobs. This sounds a bit dramatic, but in today's economic climate it is very hard to get another job in banking, as all the major banks are making people redundant.

One of the interesting effects of empires is that careers become tied to the fate of an empire. I would suggest that people who were rapidly promoted within Wholesale, and got on well with its head, could still find their career prospects hampered. Obviously, being good at your job is a factor in deciding promotions, but it was certainly not the only reason. Unless these people were noticed by another empire head (for example, by taking them out for a drink) they could find themselves side-stepped.

In a large organization there is a lot of scope to gain personal power and a high salary. Politics is, however, the name of the game. I believe that there is too much politicking within Atlantic-Pacific. There is no common goal and almost everyone is working for their own benefit. Most people are very nice to work with, but the bottom line in a company like Atlantic-Pacific is 'survival of the fittest'.

It is hard to imagine a clearer picture of an organization where, behind the facade of formal structure, a ruthless and continuous political process is going on. This is a process of empires, big and small; empires within empires; alliances; truces; diplomacy as well as open warfare. Richard's group becomes the spoils of one phase of this process, its emperor placated with a handy retirement package, its staff demoralized and fatalistic following their leader's desertion.

A critical reader of this story may raise a number of questions. Is it possible that the empires are figments of the imaginations of employees, like Richard and his colleagues? They are pawns within huge organizations, struggling to make sense of breakneck change which threatens their careers and futures; is the obsession with organizational politics, and especially its 'mean' Machiavellian dimensions, a characteristic of a Hollywood perspective on the cut-and-thrust of organizational life? In the last analysis, could Richard be indulging in a massive conspiracy theory, hatched up by his colleagues who found themselves confronted by a sensible and rational process of restructuring?

There can be little doubt that, in times of trouble and uncertainty, rumours and conspiracy theories prosper. Yet, Richard's account includes several indications that empire-building was indeed rife in Atlantic-Pacific (just as George's earlier story offers a fairly convincing argument for the existence of networks). Richard's observations of the organization's structure ('jobs appeared to have developed around the managers', some of whom led several incongruous departments, etc.) suggest that structure was the product of politics rather than expedience, rationality or expertise. His description of careers in the company indicate that the support of a champion, a backer who holds a senior position, is crucial for success (as was also the case for Helen in the Civil Service). One's career depends on 'being spotted' by an influential empire builder, who will reward personal loyalty with promotions, pay rises and honours. Finally, the fatalism and resignation of his own colleagues as they await their fate signal that they have come to see themselves as leaderless pawns, paralysed by fear. These are strong signs of a power culture, where all authority, all structure and all actions emanate from the leader.

The three stories in this chapter have highlighted the ways networks and empires can operate within organizations. Both of them cut across the formal organizational structure, and so reduce the potency of organizational rules and regulations. Both place strong emphasis on loyalty and trust. They can account for exhilarating career breakthroughs as well as for devastating reverses. They can benefit organizations by dispensing with unnecessary formalities and control, yet they can easily degenerate into arbitrariness, injustice and authoritarianism, stifling individuality and innovation. Above all, they can undermine any sense of fundamental goal or purpose, reducing organizations to territories where power is pursued for its own sake.

Thinking On

1 Ask any middle-aged graduate of a prestigious school or university if they have kept in touch with any of their classmates. Do they acknowledge the existence of a network which opened some important doors in their careers?
2 Try to imagine how James Fairclough would describe his meeting with and subsequent behaviour towards George in the first story.
3 Have you ever found yourself benefiting unexpectedly through a fortuitous coincidence? How did you feel about it?
4 Why do you think Rosemary won her confrontation with Dr Mayhew over the dismissal of Helen?
5 Have you ever striven to get noticed by someone in position of power (a teacher, a lecturer, a manager)? What tactics did you employ? Alternatively, have you ever been in a situation where you felt that survival meant not getting noticed? Contrast the two situations.

Reading On

The notion of 'network' was introduced into social science in the 1950s by Elizabeth Bott (1957) who referred to the special informal relationships that some people develop to help each other out (see also Barnes 1954). In organizations, informal networks are revealed to be a potent force in how resources are allocated, and how people gain influence and power. A compelling study by Robert Jackall (1988) shows just this, as managers go about their networking to advance their careers and personal gain – 'getting connected' with others, 'plugged into groups'.

Hosking and Fineman (1990) speak of organizational actors networking in a mobile process as they 'move around' social relations with respect to particular issues. This is the basis of politicking and empire building – which can appear particularly strange to the new employee, and alien to those who have little appetite or skill to participate.

Networking with 'in' groups can be both destructive and constructive, as Lee Iaccoca (1984) reveals from his experiences inside Ford and Chrysler. He tells of the significance of dominant cliques, families, senior managers and their lieutenants. Many authors have discussed organizational politics and empire building in organizations, including Mintzberg (1983), Pfeffer (1981) and Mangham (1986). Charles Handy (1976) has described many of the features of power culture, one of his four basic types of organizational cultures. Networks, coalitions and friendships create sources of power. Kanter (1979) and Ragins and Sundstrom (1989) discuss these processes, stressing that information links ('knowledge is power'), supply links, purchasing links, support links and friendship links all help to consolidate power, and those who actively develop their networks in one or more of these areas are more likely to gain influence. The use of networks by professional politicians is well known. Jeremy Paxman (1990) is revealing in his discussion of British old boy networks and their influence on Britain's political behaviour.

Barnes, J.A. (1954). 'Class and committees in a Norwegian island parish', *Human Relations*, 7, 1, 39–58.

Bott, E. (1957). *Family and Social Network*. London: Tavistock.

Handy, C.B. (1976). *Understanding Organizations*. Harmondsworth: Penguin.

Hosking, D. and Fineman, S. (1990). 'Organizing processes', *Journal of Management Studies*, 27, 6, 583–604.

Iaccoca, L. (1984). *Iacocca: An Autobiography*. New York: Bantam.

Jackall, R. (1988). *Moral Mazes*. New York: Oxford University Press.

Kanter, R.M. (1979). 'Power failure in management circuits', *Harvard Business Review*, 57, July–August, 65–75.

Mangham, I.L. (1986). *Power and Performance in Organizations: An Exploration of Executive Process*. Oxford: Blackwell.

Mintzberg, H. (1983). *Power In and Around Organizations*. Englewood Cliffs, NJ: Prentice Hall.

Paxman, J. (1990). *Friends in High Places: Who Runs Britain*. London: Joseph.

Pfeffer, J. (1981). *Power in Organizations*. Marshfield, MA: Pitman.

Ragins, B.R. and Sundsdrom, F. (1989). 'Gender and power in organizations: a longitudinal perspective', *Psychological Bulletin*, 105, 65.

PART 3

SURVIVAL AND INJURIES

This final part of the book tells of bruises, scars – and survival strategies.

In a way, the tone of this section is in ironical counterpoint to what many of us may regard as the way organizations *ought* to be, and indeed what some corporations claim to be: a 'family feel'; a 'strong' culture; an atmosphere of 'excellence'. Perhaps the family metaphor, in particular, is an unfortunate one to use at a time when many real families are collapsing and divorce rates in Western countries continue to climb. Real families, it seems, are places of disharmony as much as harmony; where anger, distress and a lack of caring can rip apart the best of blood ties; and the parental role is far from straightforward. And so it is with many work organizations, where those in charge cannot always lead; where organizational members can feel lost, unsupported and angry; where communication becomes difficult or devious; and where surviving the day becomes the main task at hand.

This gloomy picture of work life is brought home in a seminal work by Studs Terkel, who, with acute journalistic eye, introduces his book *Working* as follows:

> This book, being about work, is, by its very nature, about violence – to the spirit as well as to the body. It is about ulcers as well as accidents, about shouting matches as well as fistfights, about nervous breakdowns as well as kicking the dog around. It is above all (or beneath all) about daily humiliations. . . . It is about a search, too, for daily meaning as well as daily bread. (1974: 1)

Management writings are not as eloquent as Terkel's prose, although they document well the causes and consequences of stress at work. The rational content of much management education and training offers a more reassuring picture: where strong teams, *esprit de corps*, shared goals and fair dealing are presented as attainable goals, and where skilled managers are able to iron out disagreements and conflicts. But in practice, as the following pages attest, the harmony and effectiveness of the organization and its leaders are more the exceptions than the rule. Personal survival sometimes depends on being unkind rather than kind, distrustful rather than trusting. The power of some bosses is oppressive. Jobs in the most prestigious of 'excellent' organizations can be entrapping and deeply dissatisfying. Yet, to meekly accept a current culture can sometimes lead to an easier life than can be attained by challenging its inequities.

References

Terkel, S. (1974). *Working*. Penguin: Harmondsworth.

11

In at the Deep End

How do organizations receive their new employees? Joining can be a gentle, carefully-orchestrated process or a sudden immersion in deep water.

Some of the larger organizations have induction programmes to hold the new recruit's hand: courses to attend, site visits, films on the company's organization and a mentor to guide them. Given that most student trainees have not had a significant period of 'real' work, and their studies insulate them from the harsher realities of working life, a careful induction can provide a helpful transition from the world of the university or the college to the world of work.

But more common is an entry with minimal assistance and a major culture shock. Almost before they have fully crossed the organization's threshold, many new recruits are propelled into its politics. Learning happens fast, and sometimes furiously – and it does not always leave them at ease with what they discover. This is a point made by Alison, who describes how she tried to create some sense from the messages she received from her new colleagues. She worked in the Financial Services Department of a large British bank.

Alison's Story: 'A Cowboy Outfit'

At the start of my placement at Green and Farber, I had many high expectations about the world of work. I suppose I was expecting to see an efficient and professional organization in action, coupled with the prestige of working for a merchant bank.

Account Planning, as a department, is very small. It consisted of Bill (my manager), Liz and myself. Account Planning worked closely with the Financial Reporting Team – Dave (manager) and Fiona.

The first day I started work I was taken round the office and introduced by Liz. Bill was absent for that week and when Liz introduced me to Fiona she commented. 'Lucky for you, Bill's off this week. I don't think you really want to meet him.' Dave, Liz and Fiona looked at each other, laughed and then looked at me. Dave then said, 'You'll understand when you meet him.'

I felt that the way they had acted was very unprofessional. As a newcomer to the company, I felt that if the team had any differences amongst themselves, they shouldn't have been revealed to me in the first week, let alone on the first day. Without having seen Bill, I had already pre-judged him as being disliked.

A week later I met Bill. My first impression was that he seemed to be quite OK; to say he was nice would be going over the top. The use of the word 'seemed' made me think 'yes, but . . . '. Here was I, making assumptions about a person I didn't really know, which is something I object to emphatically.

The incident that really opened my eyes to the Green and Farber organization as a whole, was Bill's appraisal of Fiona. Fiona had to fill in a self-appraisal form and at the same time put forth comments about Bill's managerial style. Bill also had to complete an appraisal of Fiona. Fiona had had many 'run ins' with Bill, so she consulted Dave about how she should approach the situation. Dave informed Fiona that she should write exactly what she felt and that she was under no obligation to reveal any information to Bill prior to the actual appraisal.

A couple of days later, Bill asked Fiona if he could see her self-appraisal, so he could get an idea of her views and prepare a suitable one for her. At first Fiona refused, so Bill asked if she had something to hide. Fiona expressed to me later that she felt her hands had been 'tied'. She felt that if she refused, Bill would feel she had written something detrimental about him (which she had). However, if she handed over the appraisal, Bill would have an unfair advantage over her.

The following day Bill spoke to Fiona. He actually told her that he understood her position and to make things fair, they would swap appraisal forms. Fiona handed over her form, but Bill then said, 'I've had a word with Graham (senior manager we now worked under) and he said that there is no need for you to see what I've written before the appraisal'. In the end Fiona had quite an upsetting appraisal and left the room in tears.

I now understood why Bill was disliked by the department. Being a manager of Account Planning was the first managerial position he had held. Bill's major flaw was that he didn't seem to realize that a leader can only be a leader if others are willing to follow. Bill had the title 'manager' which he thought was all that was needed to get things done.

The incident taught me a lot about Green and Farber and the way people used their authority. Bill had no need to consult Graham about showing Fiona her appraisal. I believe he had no intention of showing the appraisal and possibly didn't even raise the issue with Graham. He just used that to get himself out of an awkward situation. Fiona went along with the situation because Bill was displaying tendencies of coercive power. Any disagreement with him could hinder her promotion chances.

The Green and Farber organization was summed up by a senior manager's joke. A wealthy Arab had three sons and he asked each of them what they wanted most of all. The first son asked for a boat, so his father bought him the QE2. The second asked for a horse, so he was bought a stable of thoroughbred stallions. The third asked for a cowboy outfit, so his dad bought him Green and Farber.

Alison was dropped well-and-truly into the deep end of the organization – straight into a tight web of office politics. In a short period of time she was introduced to a person content to besmirch a colleague's character, and to another who, it seemed, lied and double-crossed his subordinates.

For a while we see Alison struggling with herself. She was not the sort to prejudge others, she wanted to have an open mind about her new organization; yet she was suspicious of Bill after what she had heard. Indeed, when she met him she could not shake off the negative image she had received. Her immediate colleagues were keen that she shared their dislike for Bill right from the beginning – and they were successful in their early influence. Already Alison was subject to the forces of social norms – Bill was regarded as a well-deserving scapegoat, and if Alison did not fall into line with this perspective she did not truly 'belong' to the social group. Organizational socialization had begun.

When Alison heard of Fiona's difficulties and distress with Bill over the appraisal, the 'out-grouping', or demonizing, of Bill was complete. She now had evidence to back up her uncertainties, evidence which fitted well with the views of her colleagues. It also fixed her perception of the company as a less-than-professional enterprise. This view seemed endemic – jokes were told against the organization, even at senior management level. Alison now fitted in.

It is not uncommon for newcomers to encounter pressures to fall into line by 'out-grouping' a particular person or department. Identities and solidarity are often formed in adversity – against real or imagined enemies. If we are to believe Alison's account, Bill deserved much of the disapprobation heaped upon him. But we might spare a thought for the scapegoat, as it is very easy to lapse unthinkingly into stereotypes. The deviousness he displayed is not necessarily motivated by some defect of character. The Bills of the organizational world are usually insecure in their new role, anxious to cover up their weaknesses by the crude use of power. Bill would surely benefit from constructive support from his own boss if he is to begin to break the cycle of suspicion produced by his approach to management.

Frank's story, next, is one of early socialization into Imago Films, a major manufacturer of photographic materials. His impression is, very much, less negative than Alison's, making for an interesting comparison.

Frank's Story: Proud to Belong

My image of Imago, to steal a phrase, was that of a well-oiled machine. I imagined Imago, which is a market leader in photographic film, to be a strict, aggressive, formal, pin-stripe type of company. An organization which is forceful and dominant in appearance.

To my enormous surprise, my induction into the organization was one of complete informality. I was introduced to my superiors and colleagues who greeted me with smiles and handshakes aplenty. I was immediately escorted to the 'pub' and was told that this was the place where the most of the information about a particular supplier could be obtained. This information should then be used to obtain the best deal for Imago – which for most people was the ultimate goal. And indeed, after a few months I realized that people were very committed to the success of the organization, and proud to be so.

As I became more acclimatized to the working environment I began to take more notice of the framed statements from company directors which appeared on every available spare wall. The statements expressed the commitment of the company to quality and to teamwork. They stressed that the chairman was not the most important person, and neither was any one employee. The most important person was the consumer and Imago employees should be committed to their every want and need. After reading these statements, and actually observing the team spirit, who could fail to be motivated and dedicated to the company and its consumers?

Then, in my third month, Imago got involved in very serious litigation. We were being sued for a breach of copyright, and morale plummeted, as did Imago share prices. In the end we lost, and we had to pay massive compensation. But it was ruled that we had not acted intentionally or wilfully. This certainly helped. Messages were sent to newspapers and to all Imago employees that the compensation could be paid out of this year's earnings, and that the outcome, in effect, was a good one.

This result boosted morale and my image of Imago being impersonal and strict had, on the basis of the court case, finally been put to rest. I had become committed and involved, as every other employee, in the dealings of a company which we were proud to work for.

For Frank, the water in the 'deep end' of Imago was decidedly warm. There was no formal induction, but Frank floated gently and willingly in Imago's informality. Unlike Alison, he heard no schisms and was not exposed to political strife. Is this an organization where no such issues arise? We think it unlikely. Numerous reports about this company supplied by other employees paint a far darker picture.

Frank was well on the way to becoming an organizational acolyte, idealizing everything about his organization. He was fast seduced by the friendliness of his colleagues, and by the symbols of customer care and quality (sharp objectives, corporate mission statements). Such was their effect that Frank appears to have suspended his critical capacities; he accepted unqualifyingly the decency of the organization, whatever. Even the loss of a serious litigation case, a major blemish for most organizations, was reinterpreted by Frank as, in the end, showing Imago to be a fine, upstanding enterprise. His mind was made up.

Does Frank's story of his corporate socialization reveal more about Frank than about the organization? There is probably a fair measure of both. Frank does seem suggestible and somewhat starry-eyed. On the other hand, what he described illustrates the way an organization can create an atmosphere, or culture, where *feeling* positive – proud to belong – is the essential ingredient to loyalty and commitment. The style of the organization expresses the good mood, and the non-cynical employee can feel comfortable in its embrace. The actual product – be it camera film, hamburgers or lampshades – has no intrinsic good, but the company's socialization is such that it encourages people (a) to think well of the product, in high-quality terms, and (b) to think of the organization as a family where they belong, are cared for, and will be fairly rewarded. As Frank ingenuously put it, who could not want to be part of that? In fact, some people do not feel comfortable in such organizations; they feel they have been brainwashed and find it hard to express views which are contrary to the corporate 'line'.

The final story, from Denis, is set in a small firm of accountants. Denis soon experiences the unsettling feeling of being in an organization which has no place for him.

Denis's Story: A Day Out in Arsenal

It was only the second week that I had spent in the offices of Trent Spender, chartered accountants. I had no work to do. One of the partners, Trent, asked if he could sit at my desk to use the computer. Being a small practice, the only space then available for me to work in was in the 'boardroom'.

Once I had moved from my desk I asked Janice, one of the accountants, what work I should do. It was obvious that I had disturbed her and after flapping some bits of paper about she told me she had no work for me at present and that I should ask Kerry (another accountant).

Kerry dragged herself away from her files at my request for work, flapped some of her bits of paper about and gave me the same reply as Janice, nothing at the moment. She looked across to Don (the Senior Manager) and asked what I should be doing.

Don, who was always busier than Kerry and Janice put together, looked up and flapped some of his bits of paper before telling me he had nothing for me at the moment. He said I should ask Joanne (the Tax Manager) for something to do. But again, despite her large workload, she had nothing that I could be getting on with.

At this point I felt like the proverbial beachball, pushed from one employee to another. With each rejection I was becoming more deflated; I lost more and more hope and patience. However, there was one last chance – Trish the secretary. I was sure there would be some photocopying that needed to be done and that would be better than nothing. Well, I was let down even further – there was no photocopying to be done.

I returned to Trent to state my case, but before I could he told me had something very important that he would like me to do for him. He pulled out four boxes of files belonging to a client who was a printer in North London. He said the 'very important' work was to deliver the files to the client because the Inland Revenue would be visiting them. The client happened to be in Arsenal, a rather distant area of North London, home of the famous football team. It dawned on me that, having lost my space in the office, the only work they would entrust in me was as a courier. At a time when the practice was at its busiest, I faced a day out in Arsenal with no football!

This incident summed up my placement experience for several reasons. Whatever their reasons, being pushed about like a beachball from one person to the next was to become typical of my placement. I got the feeling that everyone had far more important things to do and were far too busy to sit down with me and explain how to do more demanding work. I felt that they were fobbing me off with basic duties, just for the sake of it, and passing the responsibility of providing me with work to anyone they could. It made it difficult for me to become comfortable and relaxed at work.

The whole incident that morning made me feel angry, frustrated and inadequate because they weren't giving me a proper chance to prove my capabilities. I felt as if I was in the way, under their feet, and hindering their progress – because I had to disturb them to see what task I could do next. I felt as if they would be better off with me out of the office, not causing them any disturbances. As it turned out, of course, they did manage to get me out of the office that day, and this put further doubt in my mind as to how much they really wanted and needed me.

Denis's story reads a little like a tale of perseverance from a child's story book – but without the happy ending. Denis did not receive his just reward for 'trying and trying again'. No one seemed to want him. Unlike the previous trainees, Denis remained an outsider. The organization had no way of incorporating him into its central activities or social groupings. They were too busy to throw him in at the deep end, or indeed at any end! For Denis, the pool was, figuratively speaking, empty.

He learned fast that the organization had no space for people who did not have a specific, predefined role, which would automatically bring them tasks to do. The high degree of individualism in this small, overstretched, organization of professional accountants could not easily assimilate the needs of a business student – other than for very basic tasks.

Significantly, what Denis *did* have was a place at a desk. Once he had lost this position, the sole symbol of his legitimacy and belonging, he seemed to lose all claim to a meaningful role in the organization. The organization plainly did not look after him, but it also left him in a double bind. He wanted challenging work and felt he could help out; but at the same time he felt guilty for disturbing people. Denis could be regarded as a lost resource – although that was not the way he was seen by the company.

In this chapter we have read three stories about 'entering' organizations. For Alison, joining Green and Farber was entering a world of politics, intrigue and bitterness; Frank, on the other hand, thought that he would be entering a formal, strict organization only to discover a friendly company, that he was proud to serve. Denis, in spite of his efforts, remained an outsider – the company had offered him a job but was unwilling to find him a role. All three stories generated strong initial feelings, which coloured the trainees' subsequent placement experience.

Thinking On

1   Was Denis, in the last story, really a bit of a whimp? How else might he have faced his shortage of work?
2   Think of an organization (work or non-work) that defied your initial expectations. What were the differences and how do you explain them?
3   What are the different emotional experiences people have upon joining a new organization? How do different organizations handle these feelings?
4   Reflect on your own experience of joining an organization, like a school, a firm, a university or a club. When did you actually feel that you 'belonged' to this organization? Did the organization make it easier or harder for you to feel a sense of belonging?
5   Design an ideal induction process for students entering their first work organization. You choose the type of organization.

Reading On

Some of the ways organizations impress their cultures on newcomers are indicated in the readings recommended in Part 1, especially Chapters 1, 3 and 5. Scapegoating is introduced in Chapter 9. The socialization of new employees has been discussed by Schein (1988), who argues that individuals may accept socialization and become conformist members of the organization, may rebel against it, or may adapt organizational norms to their own needs through what he terms 'creative individualism'. Hopfl (1992) has described the making of organizational acolytes very eloquently. Sims et al. (1993) discuss socialization in connection with an organization's sub- and counter-cultures, reminding us that becoming an organizational member often involves wearing more than one hat. Some of these issues are examined by Schein (1978) and Hall (1986).

The wish to belong to cohesive work-groups, which is so evident in Frank's story, has been extensively discussed by social psychologists since the pioneering Hawthorne Studies (for an extensive account, see Huczynski and Buchanan 1991). The specific role of groups and social pressures in the process of socialization is explored in social psychology texts by Brown (1986) and Myers (1994).

The present chapter also raises some social aspects of an individual's identity formation, and its stresses and anxieties. A classic text in this area is by Erikson (1968), who first coined the term 'identity crisis'; identity formation is discussed well by Hewitt (1984).

The final story in this chapter raises two important issues, alienation and territoriality. Alienation is a cornerstone of Marx's early critique of capitalism, signifying the workers' lack of control of the methods and products of their own labour. Marx intended this as a description of an objective state of affairs – so a contented car worker is no less alienated in this sense than a frustrated one. Alienation is sometimes seen, wrongly, as the opposite of job satisfaction, when in fact it stands for a broader denial of human creativity and self-realization (Marx 1975; Blauner 1964). Territoriality is addressed in textbooks by Mullins (1993) and Middlemist and Hitt (1988). In organizations, access to particular territories is strictly controlled ('authorized personnel only') and monitored through security checks. While this issue is partly covered in discussions of bureaucratic rules and regulations, these discussions rarely address the group's or individual's need for psychological and physical space. A famous study discussing the territorial claims of street gangs is by Whyte (1943). Ardrey (1967) explores the principle of territoriality in a more general way, whereas Sommer (1969) looks at its implications for the job of designers.

Ardrey, R. (1967). *The Territorial Imperative*. New York: Collins.

Blauner, R. (1964). *Alienation and Freedom*. Chicago, IL: University of Chicago Press.

Brown, R. (1986). *Social Psychology*. New York: Free Press.

Erikson, E. (1968). *Identity, Youth and Crisis*. New York: Norton.

Hall, D.T. (1986). *Career Development in Organizations*. San Francisco, CA: Jossey-Bass.

Hewitt, J. (1984). *Self and Society: A Symbolic Interactionist Social Psychology* (3rd edn). Boston, MA: Allyn and Bacon.

Hopfl, H. (1992). 'The making of the corporate acolyte', *Journal of Management Studies*, 29, 1, 23–34.

Huczynski, A. and Buchanan, D. (1991). *Organizational Behaviour* (2nd edn). London: Prentice Hall.

Marx, K. (1975). *Early Writings*. Harmondsworth: Penguin.

Middlemist, R.D. and Hitt, M.A. (1988). *Organizational Behavior*. St. Paul, MN: West.

Mullins, L.J. (1993). *Management and Organizational Behaviour* (3rd edn). London: Pitman.

Myers, D.G. (1994). *Exploring Social Psychology*. New York: McGraw-Hill.

Schein, E.H. (1978). *Career Dynamics*. Reading, MA: Addison-Wesley.

Schein, E.H. (1988). 'Organizational socialization and the profession of management', *Sloan Management Review*, reprinted in Fall 1988, pp. 53–65 (original work published in 1968).

Sims, D., Fineman, S. and Gabriel, Y. (1993). *Organizing and Organizations: An Introduction*. London: Sage.

Sommer, R. (1969). *Personal Space: The Behavioral Basis of Design*. Englewood Cliffs, NJ: Prentice Hall.

Whyte, W.F. (1943). *Street Corner Society*. Chicago, IL: University of Chicago Press.

12

Behind Closed Doors

Most organizations can point to internal procedures which are designed to assist communication – committees, reports, electronic mail, notice boards, internal television, departmental meetings.

Most of our students were exposed to such communication efforts. But some were struck by the realization that highly significant information was transmitted and shaped outside of these mechanisms. 'Facts' gained importance, and audience, as they were passed through unusual, surreptitious channels. Rumour, leaked letters and conversations behind closed doors were not just the incidental babble of organizational life, they were at the heart of its communicative and political process, and central to people's feelings about work – good and bad. To survive often meant being attuned to the whispers and gossip, and knowing what to pass on and what to 'forget'.

Just how central the unofficial communications network can be is illustrated first by Cara.

Cara's Story: A Hot Seat

On my placement I worked for Forbes Bank. It provides banking and financial products, and services to both personal and business customers. More importantly, I worked in Central Operations Finance which is the business support unit responsible for the preparation of the monthly accounts and budgets for all the principal areas of Forbes.

Incredibly, I was sitting on the toilet at the time. I'd almost finished when I heard the door open and two people walk in. I knew it was two because of the unmistakeable sound of stilettos. Unfortunately it was my boss Ula and her secretary Hannah.

I'd like to conjure up for you an image of Ula. She is rude, swears every other word, and in my eyes not an ideal manager. But she is effective, a superb negotiator and has twelve men always trying to charm her. Ula was furious about something. I didn't make a sound. This is what I heard.

Yesterday she had had a meeting with Bobby Shand, who is Head of Finance, and the Card Operations manager. After the meeting Bobby and Ula were informally discussing a point from the meeting (Ula's relationship with Bobby can be summed up in a song, 'I want to be Bobby's girl'; she is often seen toadying up to him in subtle ways). What they had been discussing was the budget. Briefly, every department has to recover their costs from other departments that have used their services. We were under-recovering and Card Operations were going to be our scapegoat as we were going to overcharge them, unknown to us and them!

Eric is one the line managers in Ula's team. He is extremely clever and analytical but lacks any kind of finesse, tact, poise or diplomacy. Regrettably for him, his desk is by Ula's office entrance. He had heard every word of this 'unofficial' conversation. He then went off and, plainly, talked to the wrong person about it. The 'scandal' reached Card Operations manager. It was meant to be confidential between Ula and Bobby. Evidently the Card Operations manager's immediate reaction was to get on the telephone to ask Bobby 'What the hell are you playing at?' Bobby's counter-reaction was to get on the telephone and chide Ula. It was now her fault, because Eric was one of her team. She would have to discipline him. She was fuming with Eric for using the information in a 'crass and unprofessional manner'.

My initial reaction was how tactless she was being for talking this way in the toilets. I could have been anyone. I feel it was crude of me, like Eric, to listen to Ula in this way. But I was intrigued and too afraid to move. Ula would have known I had heard every word and she could have made my life very complicated. In retrospect I wish I had left, proving to her I could have been anyone and that I had heard every word!

*After Ula had calmed down she decided to talk to Eric about 'not discussing information privately and casually with people outside the department'. I thought '**What rubbish!**', Ula (and most of Forbes) have made half their deals by doing exactly this and now she was going to discipline someone for doing the same thing. It usually works for Ula, but this time it was going to have a very detrimental effect on the department and our relationship with Card Operations.*

Forbes is a very cloudy culture. There might be many written rules about how things are done, but something very different happens at the implementation stage. To survive and be successful, like I wanted to, you have to subconsciously write your own manual of rules. As I've shown, these ways might not always be legitimate. The power really remains with the 'chats down the pub' or the corridor meetings. You need to adapt, read the unwritten signals of your work mates, 'do as we do'.

Cara's account is something of a triple-take. First she overheard Ula, her boss, divulging to her secretary a secret plot. Secondly, that very plot is overheard by a third party resulting in the plan dramatically misfiring. And thirdly, Cara found herself in exactly the 'snooping' role that is denounced by her boss. Cara wavered a little, in a moral quandary at her unexpected lavatorial position. But, as she rationalized in the end, this was a model for how things were done in Forbes; it was the unwritten signals that were the ones to attend to if one was to 'survive and be successful'.

This story reveals the intensity, force and passion that can fuel the generation and transmission of gossip and innuendo. It also shows, very plainly, that some organizations cultivate that particular style of operating, soon to be picked up by the astute newcomer. When business is done in quiet corners, bypassing the formal channels of communication, it breeds secrecy and suspicion. The formal procedures become a mask, beneath which the real work is done. And those who listen most carefully to the sighs and whispers have most chance of success – or at least of avoiding undue injury.

Like many of the issues highlighted in this book, it would be unrealistic to assume that this facet of the organization's underbelly is 'all wrong'. Academic researchers have shown that it is very hard to envisage any social organization without a grapevine of communication. What is manageable, however, is the tone and structure of the organization's communicative culture, so that the whispers and secrecy can be less of a preoccupation.

Natalie's story, which follows, contrasts with Cara's in that it takes place in a small organization. Nevertheless, the effects of conducting clandestine conversations were no less significant – nor were their consequences.

Natalie's Story: Walls Have Ears

R. Randle & Sons is a precision engineering firm in Glasgow. It is a relatively small company employing forty people, who are involved in the design and making of rubber moulds which eventually produce seals for car doors.

*I was witness to several heated discussions between the manag-
ing director and the general manager, Tim. Tim acted as the
spokesman for the other office staff, except for the company
accountant, Roger. He was a 'yes' man – 'he knew which side his
bread was buttered' and thus agreed with the managing director
in every respect. This was even to the sacrifice of respect from his
colleagues.*

*The managing director's office was offset from the main
building, in a Portakabin. There, he and Roger often spent several
hours a day talking. My office adjoined the managing director's; I
openly heard most conversations. I would estimate that 20 per cent
of this time was spent discussing business. The remainder
included social interests and various character assassinations. It
shortly became clear to me that there was a strong desire to
diminish Tim's authority, in the hope he would find a job
elsewhere and leave. It was also hoped that Irene, a receptionist,
could be 'encouraged to leave'. Irene was the sister of the former
owner, and a lingering reminder of the old-style company. The rest
of the staff had a good idea that the continuous discussions
between Roger and the managing director were not simply
concerning company finances. They resented the time they spent in
this way and became hostile and suspicious. Morale plummeted.*

*The managing director's solution to his staff problems was to
announce a restructuring of the company. Each member of the
'white collar' staff was individually summoned to his office and
told about their new positions. Not surprisingly to me, only Tim
and Irene were disadvantaged. Tim was demoted from general
manager to service manager, the factory manager was to take over
about 30 per cent of his previous responsibilities. Irene's hours
were to be halved.*

*At the end of the morning, the managing director entered my
office, smiling and rubbing his hands. Referring to Tim he said,
'He took it well, he was mostly upset with losing the car and petrol',
and laughed.*

*The consequence of all this was dramatic deterioration in
staff–management relations. Tempers frayed. There was little
trust and a growing disrespect. Morale was rock bottom, free
overtime and company loyalty became things of the past. The other
staff did not like how the whole matter was conducted, especially
the way Irene and Tim were treated.*

*I felt uncomfortable that I knew about the plotting and
scheming, and Roger's two-faced remarks before the others. I did
not want to be perceived 'as one of them' just because my office was*

'over there'. Thankfully, I was seen as a harmless fly on the wall since I found both sides confided and trusted in me. I felt sorry for the victims of the plot and frustrated that I too was powerless to help them. I selfishly found it important to remain neutral. From a practical stance, I would have been alienated had I taken sides, even though I had strong views. I would have lost the trust of my managers and this would have severely disadvantaged my placement.

This story shows that once the sense grows that something is being plotted behind closed doors, it is then hard to uproot the seedlings of suspicion. Mistrust of management soon spreads, undermining any feeling of cooperation or trust.

It could also be argued that the managing director was simply a poor Machiavellian. He clearly had not accounted for the image to the workforce of the long meetings in his office, nor had he reflected on the inadequate soundproofing of his office. Finally, his 'victory' was a pyrrhic one – at least in the short term: staff resentment and loyalty were at rock bottom. Tim and Irene were obvious casualties, and it would be surprising if they were not feeling considerably hurt – in ways the MD chose not to see or convey.

Natalie, like Cara in the first story, was ambivalent about her role as unexpected witness to a plot. She did not want to be identified with such nefarious dealings, and she sheltered behind her student status. In the end, though, she exhibited a self-interest common to many nervous organizational members: if a principle is worth standing up for, think about your job first.

The last story is by Sophie, who was a trainee in a large computer and software manufacturer, Radcom. Her story takes place at a time when speculation about redundancies was rife.

Sophie's Story: Leaky Channels

At the beginning of the third week of February, rumours began to circulate about an official announcement which was likely to take place later in the week. Tensions began to mount and rumours about redundancies were rife. Some were even saying that the whole site was to be closed.

On Thursday morning there was as an e-mail sent to all employees giving them details of the time and location of departmental meetings at which important announcements were to be made. At that time at least five members of the department were away skiing, including my direct boss and Bryn, the other Bath student. I checked my mailbox, but had received nothing significant. I thought that it might be a mistake. About 15 minutes before the meeting I decided to go and ask Mick Yates, head of the department, if I was invited or not, as lots of people in my department were asking me if I was nearly ready to go. Mick said that I wasn't invited because the announcement wouldn't affect me. It was against company policy to invite industrial trainees, and as a consequence it would be inappropriate for me to attend. He said that he would tell me all about it afterwards, so that I knew what was happening.

By this time, however, I already knew most of what was going to be announced (and quite a lot which wasn't going to be!) through the informal gossip channels. My main source of information was Fran, Mick Yates' secretary, with whom I had become very friendly. She had the unenviable responsibility of knowing what was going to happen to people before they knew themselves. She told me that Mick Yates had been promoted.

I sat alone in the large, open plan office, whilst everyone else was at the meeting. Later that day Mick gave me the official announcement which had, of course, already been related to me by my colleagues.

*On reflection, I was really surprised that I wasn't invited to the announcement as I felt that I was being excluded from the department. This was very upsetting as I was usually treated as, and felt, a full member of our team. In one fell swoop Mick had managed to inform me that I was an **outsider** and didn't really belong. I felt that this contradicted the company policy towards industrial trainees, which was to integrate them fully into the department so that both parties could gain as much as possible. I can see why Tim didn't invite me; he was unsure how other members of the department would react and in this situation it is better to be safe than sorry! However, had he spent more time on the site I'm sure he would have realized that I had been fully accepted as a **normal** member of the group. (In fact, even my direct boss needed reminding every now and then that I was a student and would only be there for a few more months!)*

That week was a real eye-opener for me regarding informal communication networks. There were a lot of leaks in the formal channels. These caused so many rumours and secrets, which in turn created bad feelings and an 'us versus them' atmosphere. Lots of people were secretly writing CVs, constantly looking over their shoulders. This completely conflicted with the positive, open image of the company, which was communicated through the official channels. What were once loyal and proud employees were becoming cynical and bitter about the company. I felt so guilty that my job was completely secure whilst people who had worked there for years, with families and mortgages, were facing the risk and in some cases the reality of being without a job. However, no one in my department seemed to hold this against me, although there was a general negative feeling towards industrial trainees.

You know, despite all the bad feelings and suspicions caused by redundancies, etc., Radcom has held together, and will continue to as long as the situation does not worsen too much. There is a strong **usness** *about Radcom employees even when things are going badly. This is still with me now, and when I see Radcom machines. I feel proud and think '***We sell those***' and feel that I was really part of it.*

Yet again, we see the socially destructive effects of rumour, as well as the way it can bolster some people's power and position. When personal uncertainty and anxiety is high, such as in a redundancy situation, uncontrolled communication can be explosive and dramatic ('the whole site will close'). Rumour will beget rumour and, given the absence of any other authoritative source, it is the truth to which people will respond. Sophie revealed how divisive this could be as people became suspicious of 'them', the management, and started looking for ways out of the company.

For Sophie, personally, being excluded from a major 'communication' event caused her much inner conflict. On the one hand she felt part of the Radcom team, but the exclusion left her feeling not so sure. Like students in other stories, she felt uneasy when she saw that people's careers were at stake – but not hers. She could understand why she might be excluded from the announcement of redundancies, but still resented what was, in her eyes, a snub – consistent with the low status of trainees in the company. It is uncomfortable to no longer feel you 'belong'. Yet, it attests to the strength of Radcom's socialization of Sophie that she still feels a buzz of pride when seeing Radcom's products.

At some levels, the manipulation of information – who discloses what to whom – becomes something of a game, but a serious game. 'Tight' confidences are swapped, to reappear in slightly different guises elsewhere. A psychological feature of rumour is that, whatever its source, after passing through a number of hands it will end up transformed. Each transmission will strip it of some of its original contextual detail.

In Sophie's organization, like many organizations, the senior manager's secretary was a central and powerful player. She (rarely he) is usually a funnel for many communications and often knows about issues before many other people do. If she opens her boss's mail and takes phone messages, she is the first to be privy to confidences. Thus Fran, the secretary, knew what was going to happen before the key meeting. But Fran was a 'leaky channel', and told her friend Sophie the result before the match, so to speak. In this way, Sophie's exclusion from the formal communication meeting was ameliorated somewhat; Sophie was still 'in'. But what was not ameliorated was the 'cynical and bitter' legacy of the communication fiasco throughout the company.

Thinking On

1 Think of examples of damaging rumours. How did they occur? Why were they damaging?
2 Was Cara right in staying put in her 'hot seat'? What would you have done, and why?
3 In one way or another, could all the students in this chapter be regarded as accomplices to rumour or plotting?
4 Do you think that some managers may deliberately put out rumours, through their secretaries or other subordinates? What functions would such a tactic serve? What are its dangers?
5 If you ran an organization, how would you design and implement a communication system which had minimum leaks?

Reading On

The broad principles of communication – psychological and structural – are laid out in most introductory texts on organizational behaviour, such as Hellriegel et al. (1995) and Daft (1995). These works examine different models of interpersonal communication, silent (non-verbal) communication, gender differences, networks of communications, and the role of information technologies. Some of the early studies on communication (e.g. Bavelas 1950; Leavitt 1951) used laboratory methods to determine which shapes of network (circle, chain, 'Y', wheel) were more accurate, faster or happier for participants. Such designs may be applicable to some highly structured work situations, but they have been criticized for their artificiality (Farce et al. 1977). Communication is revealed to be multi-faceted, multichannelled and complexly embedded in the organization's social processes.

The relationship between organizational change, politics and culture is covered in more specialist volumes, such as Fischer (1993), Pepper (1995) and Stohl (1995). These authors discuss informal channels, showing how they can compete with, or even replace, more formal designs. In this sense, informal networks can be subversive, undermining the direction and changes desired by management. But in doing so they often release, or express, the concerns of employees who feel constrained by the formal structure of communication. The grapevine is part of this. Although the grapevine is often associated with unfounded rumour, it grows from people's spontaneous desire to communicate and penetrate security screens. Research specifically on the grapevine can be found in the writings of Vickery (1984) and Davis (1969). This suggests that, contrary to common wisdom, grapevine information is true more often than not, even though it is reshaped as it travels along the 'vine'. Furthermore, Sutton and Porter (1968) note how well organizational members can often predict how information will spread – and who will do the spreading.

Bavelas, A. (1950). 'Communication in task oriented teams', *Journal of Acoustical Society of America*, 22, 725–30.

Daft, R.L. (1995). *Organization Theory and Design*. Minneapolis/St Paul, MN: West.

Davis, K. (1969). 'Grapevine communication among lower and middle managers', *Personnel Journal*, April, 269–72.

Farce, R.E., Monge, P.R. and Russell, H.M. (1977). *Communicating and Organizing*. Reading, MA: Addison-Wesley.

Fischer, D. (1993). *Communication in Organizations*. Minneapolis/St Paul, MN: West.

Hellriegel, D., Slocum, J.W. and Woodman, R.W. (1995). *Organizational Behavior*. Minneapolis/St Paul, MN: West.

Leavitt, H. (1951). 'Some effects of certain communication patterns on group performance', *Journal of Abnormal and Social Psychology*, 46, 38–59.

Pepper, G.L. (1995). *Communication in Organizations: A Cultural Approach*. New York: McGraw-Hill.

Stohl, C. (1995). *Organizational Communication: Connectedness in Action*. Thousand Oaks, CA: Sage.

Sutton, H. and Porter, L.W. (1968). 'A study of the grapevine in a governmental organization', *Personnel Psychology*, 21, 223–30.

Vickery, H.B. (1984). 'Tapping into the employee grapevine', *Association Management*, January, 36, 56–63.

13

Injuries and Insults

Life is full of injuries and insults, so it would be strange if organizations were substantially different. Yet our students did not expect the degree of injury or insult they witnessed. They would observe practices, minor and major, where employees were treated with discourtesy or disdain. Sometimes the students themselves were the victims, which was especially difficult given that they were under the organization's stewardship. They would struggle to understand what was happening, as well as where, and how, to express their feelings.

Such events underscore the fact that organizational life is often based on a set of role relationships, procedures and expectations where the emotional costs are not counted, and where the expression of certain feelings is seen to interfere with task performance. People can find it hard to know where to 'place' out-of-role feelings – such as compassion, loss, anger or hurt. Furthermore, the organization will often respond to personal distress in the only way it knows how – bureaucratically; establishing routine procedures for handling grievances, disputes or 'stress'. The visible display of such emotions must be contained, so that normal service can be resumed as soon as possible.

The three stories we report typify some of the distress which students experienced directly, or witnessed, during their placements. The first, recounted by Patricia, shows how a fairly simple organizational ritual in a publishing company grew to be major ordeal for her – but nobody seemed to notice. Elena's account concerns the handling of redundancies – an area, as we have already noted, that upset many students. Finally, Roopak tells a traumatic story of the death of a colleague, and the crude organizational response to cover the traces.

Patricia's Story: Crumbs of Comfort

'That which is everybody's business is nobody's business'. (Isaac Walton)

In the Netherlands it is traditional on one's birthday to give everyone in your office (and relatives and friends) cakes. It dates back from when the Dutch used to keep an 'open house' on their birthday, with tea, cakes and hospitality to anyone passing by. In Swift Publishing, where I worked, the cake ritual lived on. Various peoples' birthdays had passed and dutifully each person had taken the cake orders of all fellow employees (there were around twenty people in my office and fifteen more in the office further down the road). The cake shop favoured by everyone was an expensive patisserie about five minutes walk from the office. The cost to you on your birthday of this 'treat' was around fifty pounds. For most people in the company this is not so important whilst on such a high salary. For a student on a wage of seventy-five pounds a week it was a nightmare.

My birthday got closer and closer. I dropped hints about offering everyone home-made cakes. There were a lot of disapproving looks exchanged between workmates, and a few 'well, if it has to be, I suppose . . .'. Other comments were 'that's rather brave of you', 'oh, that will be **different**'.

The dreaded day came closer, and then, what a relief, Rees (my manager) asked me to travel with him to Belgium on my birthday. With a smile of great relief I warned the sales support department (the core of my office) that I would, after all, be away.

'Oh', said Netta brightly, 'that's OK; you will just have to buy the cakes and drop them off before you leave – or give them out when you come back. We can't miss the cakes.'

Rees, a few days later, called off the trip, as he was prone to do. He was always a very busy man.

I begged the help of as many people as I could, but they were away at the time or busy that evening. The evening before arrived. I had all the ingredients I needed, and a whole lot more that I probably didn't need.

The first cake was mixed and put in the pre-heated oven. In five minutes a very distinct burning smell was coming from the oven. A disaster, the top burnt in five minutes. The oven had only one temperature (it was a very old gas oven) and this temperature seemed more appropriate to firing earthenware pots.

The next attempt was a chocolate cake translated from a Dutch recipe (I had no English recipe book). Even though numerous little prayers were offered to anyone who wished to hear them, this came out like cardboard and no amount of cutting could slice it. Well, as you can probably guess the last cake was a disaster, also.

It was eight in the evening and there was a very desperate

English person in Amsterdam. I had just resigned myself to the fact that I was going to be quite a lot poorer the next day when I remembered that it was late night shopping. I ran to the local department store and bought two cakes that looked the most authentically home-cooked.

After scraping the worst burnt parts off the apple cake (the first attempt), and with fingers crossed, I set off to work with the three cakes. Careful positioning of the apple cake made the top less noticeable, and off I went on my rounds.

Well, a few thanks here and there but no real appreciation. Nobody realized that they were not home-made, and so could not be disappointed that I had not bothered to get their favourites. I was very upset and stressed. Even though everyone realised my position, they would still have found it unacceptable for me to buy-in ready-made cakes or to offer them something different. Sometimes, even in a relatively small company, it is almost impossible to bring changes until they are forced on people.

The company had started with a few people and has now more than doubled in size. Traditions started three or four years ago, such as a glass of wine on a Friday lunchtime, have long since died. No one can make the time now. Traditions such as the cakes continue, but have lost the pleasantness that was supposed to be the whole idea behind them. People expect them, and not only that, they could not accept anything 'inferior'. They have built an image up around themselves that in these matters they cannot or will not adapt to new circumstances.

Patricia's growing unease about 'delivering the cakes' was, it would seem, well signalled to her colleagues. But the ritual was such that few seemed to notice her growing panic. No one offered to help her out. It was her turn, and that was that; the 'rules' were clear. So an ostensibly fun affair turned into tyranny for one rather impoverished student. The injury was taking hold and social pressures were locking Patricia into a course of action that was unavoidable. Her embarrassment would be too great simply to refuse to take part.

But many people find themselves embarrassed into situations without feeling overwhelmed by the pressures. Patricia's sensitivity to 'having to do the right thing' suggests that we cannot discount personality effects in understanding the nature of injury. What feels a fairly inconsequential demand to one person is putting one's self-esteem on the line to another.

It could also be that Patricia's colleagues' lack of concern for her plight was less innocent than it appears. Netta's 'bright' response, reminding Patricia of her obligations, could have been a way of 'scoring' over Patricia. How well-liked was Patricia? The difficulty Patricia experienced was no mortal blow, but forcing the cake ritual would be one way of disguising an attack on her. The fact that Patricia's efforts were received with muted enthusiasm is consistent with this interpretation. Alternatively, as Patricia herself suggests, the tradition may have simply lacked depth – as long as it happened, no one complained. Patricia would have to keep her feelings of being insulted to herself.

Elena's story, next, is from her time in one of the largest UK banks. It takes injury and insult to a rather deeper level.

Elena's Story: Redundant

It is Wednesday morning, the time is 10 o'clock and the place is Group Chief Accountants Department, Northern Bank Head Office. We are in the middle of our daily morning meeting. Everything is as usual and all the members of the board reporting team are present – David (the senior manager), Paul (my manager), Sue, Phil, Andrew, Frank and myself. We are discussing progress, deadlines and changes, but also issues of more personal character as we all know each other quite well by now.

Twenty-four hours later – the place is the same and so are the people present, but not for very much longer. Rick, the head of our department, has just explained that there will be some 'slight' changes to our department. Phil and Andrew have been made redundant. Sue has to take on another job in the bank due to the reorganization, and Paul has had his application for voluntary redundancy accepted. What is left of the 'we' is David, Frank and me. Considering the fact that David as senior manager only attends some of the meetings, and Frank has just joined the team, I am effectively the most experienced member of the team. Not my idea of minor changes!

Looking around the conference room I see sad and shocked faces. Phil and Andrew had no idea that they would be made redundant. They have both been with the bank all of their working life, and thought this would make them safe. Sue, who is the one I have been working most closely with, has to take on a job she does not want.

However, it is the fact that Paul is leaving that upset me the most. Who is going to be there to explain and help me when they are all gone? The natural answer would be David, but he is only sitting around laughing – the only way he knows to approach a problem. He is so disorganized that he cannot even look after himself. The result of all this is that I am going to be in charge of myself; there is not going to be anyone to help me out.

Northern had just been taken over when I joined. Therefore the fear of redundancy was present in the department from the day I joined. There was also a feeling of having been neglected by the management, especially by the lack of information being passed downwards. This caused uncertainty as no one knew what would happen and what the effects would be. The only information available would be what I heard through the grapevine. It was therefore, in many ways, better when people had been told about the redundancies and everyone had some clear facts to relate to.

Another cause of frustration was that the redundancies seemed to have been decided on a very random basis. It did not seem like management had given any thought to the human and practical perspectives. How can a team be expected to perform its best when it has been more than halved? Things would have been easier if we had been approached by management and told that they were aware of the difficulties we were facing. But they just expected us to go on as if nothing had changed. What scared me the most was that, not only did I have to do my own tasks without supervision, but I also had to take on most of my manager's tasks. I was not ready for all the responsibility involved.

The fact that I was a placement student put me in an awkward position. The people who had been made redundant were more or less blaming me for having taken their jobs. The general attitude in the department had been that they should not take on placement students while they were laying-off staff. I can understand their way of thinking. But the worst thing was not the blame, but that people who I knew quite well after four months of working together, did not want to know me. I was not allowed to show them the sympathy I felt.

Earlier, the working atmosphere in the department had been very friendly; now it was an 'us and them' attitude, against the management. My problem was that I was neither regarded as 'us' nor 'them'. I was just a placement student who would be leaving shortly and escape all problems. No one seemed to realize that I was also concerned by what was happening, and that it was affecting my work as well.

'It did not seem like the management had given any thought to the human and practical perspectives . . .', says Elena. It is hard to resist the conclusion that she was probably right. In many large takeovers (and less grand 'restructuring' attempts), it is often wider financial criteria and the interests of remote stakeholders in the organization which drive the decisions.

People become pawns, moved by seemingly invisible hands. The extent to which top management builds in support for those directly affected by such changes varies. Often it is a token measure – such as 'outplacement' counselling for the redundant and redeployment for some. In Northern, it seemed to be each person for him or herself.

Certainly, such events challenge the soothing claims of a corporation's human resource philosophy. As Elena and her colleagues were to find, the protective umbrella of the bank was myth, and loyalty and long-term service offered little security. This has been a common experience for those living through the recessions of the 1980s and 90s, and is likely to continue as corporations seek different ways of surviving in highly competitive markets. But the irresistible message from Elena's type of experience is that organizational survival also depends on members of the organization feeling reasonably secure and trusting their management in *all* circumstances. A heavy-handed approach in times of crisis can undermine the firm's economic survival because of the demotivating effect on those who are left to run affairs.

In Elena's department, the recipe for social and psychological damage was almost perfect. A long period of uncertainty and rumour, fuelling anxiety. Then a sudden hatchet job, with no apparent rationale and no appeal. There were winners and there were losers – or perhaps everyone was a loser. A comfortable working team was decimated, yet the remaining team members were still expected to carry on.

Elena herself felt trapped, guilt-ridden and lonely. She survived the shake out, but only because she had a temporary job. She wanted to offer support and sympathy, but found herself a focus of resentment. Why should she, a student, have a job while others in greater need lost theirs? Elena became an object of some animosity – she was there, unwittingly, a symbol of the difficulties generated by those much higher up in the organization. They could not be influenced, but Elena could be; a scapegoat for her colleagues' bad feelings.

The final story is recounted by Roopak, who worked in the Treasury Department of an international chain of hotels. Elena and her colleagues had to absorb the implications of the decimation of their department; Roopak had to face an actual death.

Roopak's Story: The Death of Jim Gerrard

The ritual of what I came to call 'Jim bashing' began on my very first day at the Treasury Department of Hotelworld. Jim Gerrard was a very unpopular leader. Jim had a very serious drink problem which seriously affected his performance at work. Within Treasury there was a constant cover-up operation whereby they were constantly trying to make excuses for his lack of professionalism. Especially, this applied to Jim's secretary who, during the day, would fend-off several irate clients who were wondering why Jim had failed to keep an appointment twice in a row. Apart from such excuses, Jim was not discussed with anyone outside Treasury.

That Friday he had been invited by Stornforth Bank to spend the day at a football match. I wished him a good day and said I would see him on Monday. That afternoon Jim's secretary received a strange phonecall from Stornforth Bank. Did we know where Jim was? He had left his seat at half-time to visit the toilet and had not returned. Furthermore, he had left his briefcase behind. Five minutes later, Jim phoned. He was at home; he offered no explanation for his earlier behaviour. Could we courier his briefcase to his home when we received it? We agreed.

Just as we were all leaving for the weekend the courier returned, and with him the now infamous briefcase. There had been no reply from Jim's house. We were all astounded by Jim's behaviour that day which was bizarre, even by his standards. His secretary was at breaking point now, and said she would 'sort out this bloody mess on Monday'.

I arrived in the office the next Monday to find a rather subdued atmosphere. My boss, Dave, immediately took me aside and said,

'Roopak. I have some very bad news to tell you.'
'Oh no, don't tell me. I've got the sack', I joked.
'No Roopak. This is serious. Jim died over the weekend.'

I was stunned by the news. 'How did it happen?', I asked. Nobody knew, but there was a real feeling that something was being held back from us all. Just as we had covered for Jim whilst he was alive, others were covering for him now. I sensed my colleagues in the office were in a dilemma. There was no denying that they deeply disliked Jim, so how should they act now that he was gone? There was no genuine grief, for that would have been sheer hypocrisy. But neither did the department feel they could act as if nothing had happened. Nobody would have wished it upon him, and some, I think, felt a twinge of guilt that they didn't have the courage to put their necks on the line and take the issue up with someone. 'Maybe he just needed help', someone remarked.

Thus, at lunch that day, the Treasury Department found themselves in an awkward situation. Predictably, we were now the focus of the whole company and everywhere we turned we were greeted by sympathetic smiles. Treasury, under the microscope, had to act grief-stricken. Anything else, to those outside the department who were unaware of the internal situation, would have seemed wholly inappropriate. Thus, we acted in the manner we were expected to act, even though some people were betraying their true feelings.

Very soon the efficient wheels of Hotelworld were in full swing. Jim's death was a messy incident and rather embarrassing to the company. The same day we were told of his death his office was turned upside down by internal auditors, making sure he hadn't misused any company money in the days before his death. There was something very clinical about the way the whole incident was being treated by senior management. I felt it was almost just another piece of business executed in the Hotelworld way; with speed, efficiency and shrouded in secrecy.

But this secrecy backfired. Speculation as to cause of death was rife and got to the point when the management had to 'come clean' with everyone. On the Saturday night, Jim had hung himself at his home. This may have quelled the gossip, but the Hotelworld machine rolled on. What shocked me the most was how soon a power struggle within the company broke out for Jim's job. Soon, people were even joking with me that he had been fine for years before my arrival, but two weeks of me had driven the poor man to suicide. Perhaps the humour was just a way of coping with shock, or even just something to say. I even found myself joking that I was annoyed that Jim had given me a project to do, and not bothered to wait around to see it finished. Although I had only known him two weeks, and so I wasn't truly upset, I used the humour to alleviate the shock, and just take away some of the general awkwardness about the whole thing that I felt.

Some of the emotion-words that Roopak uses are revealing – 'awkwardness', 'embarrassment', 'act grief-stricken'. Here was the tragic and dramatic death of a manager; social protocol demanded at least a semblance of grief and respect, but it was a grief that no one really felt and a respect that was paper thin. Jim Gerrard was regarded as an all-round nuisance, making people's work-lives difficult or intolerable. He was a heavy drinker who could no longer pull his weight. He had to be 'worked around' and hushed up.

But the manner of his death exposed three things. First, feelings of moral poverty among Jim's staff. The individual with overt 'personal problems' in an organization often feels, and is received, like a displaced person. Counselling services are rarely available, and most management systems have neither the skill nor the will to address difficulties such as alcoholism. Colleagues were embarrassed, so as far as possible the issue was ignored; there was a conspiracy of silence. It was only after the suicide that people realized they had done nothing to acknowledge, or positively to respond to, another human being's unhappiness.

Secondly, after just a short period of feigned mourning, the shocking image of the suicide was psychologically distanced – through black humour. This helped Roopak and others to cope with their awkwardness; humour is a splendid tension breaker. It is arguable whether this form of behaviour would have occurred if Jim had been well liked. To an outsider, such humour borders on the insulting.

Finally, the agents of organizational control – internal auditors – transformed Jim's memory into a bureaucratic blip. Jim's financial propriety was their concern. For the organization to continue, the books had to be straightened. Jim had embarrassed everyone enough already.

The stories in this chapter show that injuries and insults may grow from relatively small organizational happenings (the cakes) or major traumas (redundancy, a suicide). Offence for some people can lie in a casual or careless remark from a boss or colleague, while others seem inured to such innuendo. It is not uncommon for people to harbour a sense of injustice, grudge or hurt after such an encounter, which can turn into a major source of personal stress and resentment. But because organizations are tied together in status and power relationships, it is hard for individuals to express openly their distress or pique – without fear of compromise or retribution.

Insult can also be set within the institution's culture, or bureaucratic response. The second and third stories amply illustrate this. Some organizations do not know how to handle some of the most crucial human issues. So redundancies and death are treated as unfeeling events, to be managed – in part or in whole – like any other work procedure. This is not to suggest that such lack of care is necessarily deliberate. Executives, who are themselves anxious about the sensitive ground they are treading on, can hide beneath rules and procedures. If they feel some guilt as well (such as their own indirect role in a redundancy or death), they may seek added protection. But the consequent injury to people's reputation, self-esteem or memory is not measured; the negative effect on trust and morale is not costed.

Thinking On

1   Should Hotelworld have done more for Jim when he was alive? What do you think about Roopak's role?
2   Can you think of organizations that really care about the people who work for them? What makes them so special?
3   Patricia, in the first story, found herself trapped by other peoples' expectations of her. In what ways could she have handled the situation differently?
4   Have you, or someone you know, felt injured by the treatment received at the hands of an employer. What were the feelings involved, and the reasons for those feelings?
5   What coping mechanisms do people employ in overcoming insults and injuries endured at the workplace?

Reading On

Feeling injured or hurt is examined in psychodynamic writings about work, such as those by Hirschhorn (1988), Gabriel (1991) and Kets de Vries (1991). The approach of these writers is that felt injuries are more than here-and-now phenomena. They represent a rekindling or re-enactment of past injuries or unacknowledged fears. These may concern parental or other authority figures, fears about failure or about preserving self-esteem. Because the past events were painful, they have been suppressed or repressed, so the individual is unaware of their influence when he or she engages with similar occurrences or relationships at work.

The psychodynamic approach focuses on the individual and his or her early life experiences. Sennett and Cobb (1973) take a more sociological, or social class, position. They argue that when people have to accept that they are constantly given orders, they adjust by disparaging themselves, secretly ashamed of what they are. Purcell (1982) speaks of women factory workers becoming fatalistic, a hidden injury of their subordinate social position.

The uncertainties and stresses created by the restructuring of organizations and redundancy are addressed by a number of different researchers – for example, Hartley et al. (1991), Fineman (1983, 1987) and Golzen and Garner (1990). They show two things. First, that the process of redundancy, how it is managed by the organization, is often crude or brutal – and leaves its scars. Job uncertainty can infect an organization's culture to such an extent that those who are, in fact, relatively secure in their jobs stop feeling that way. They will respond by over-performing (to try and preserve their position), under-performing (from demoralization), or seeking a job elsewhere. Secondly, that people who sink their identity in their job are extremely threatened by the prospect or actuality of unemployment, and adjustment is akin to a bereavement. Full recovery does not necessarily occur when finding a new job.

Fineman, S. (1983). *White Collar Unemployment*. Chichester: Wiley.

Fineman, S. (1987). *Unemployment: Personal and Social Consequences*. London: Tavistock.

Gabriel, Y. (1991). 'Organizations and their discontents: a psychoanalytic contribution to the study of corporate culture', *Journal of Applied Behavioural Science*, 27, 318–36.

Golzen, G. and Garner, A. (1990). *Smart Moves*. Oxford: Blackwell.

Hartley, J., Jacobson, D., Klandermans, B. and Van Vuuren, T. (eds) (1991). *Job Insecurity*. London: Sage.

Hirschhorn, L. (1988). *The Workplace Within: Psychodynamics of Organizational Life*. Cambridge, MA: MIT Press.

Kets de Vries, M.F.R. (ed.) (1991). *Organizations on the Couch: Clinical Perspectives on Organizational Behavior and Change*. San Francisco, CA: Jossey-Bass.

Purcell, K. (1982). 'Female manual workers: fatalism and the reinforcement of inequity', in Robbins, D. (ed.), *Rethinking Inequality*. Aldershot: Gower.

Sennett, R. and Cobb, J. (1973). *The Hidden Injuries of Class*. New York: Vantage Books.

14

Sexual Harassment

Personal life and sexuality are not simply left behind in the company car park. They influence everyday attitudes and feelings at work – subtly and directly, consciously and unconsciously. Unwanted sexual attention, or harassment, has now become part of the public agenda of organizational life. Rather than something to be suppressed for fear of recrimination or ridicule, there is now a more open appreciation that sexual harassment is an outrage, and that organizations should take formal measures to prevent it. Not long ago, the image of the male boss pinching the female secretary's bottom was seen as acceptable fodder for film and television soap operas, as well as actual boss–secretary encounters. Now, this would be judged as not only politically incorrect, but an affront to the secretary and an abuse of male and managerial power.

Sexual harassment raises many difficult questions – most fundamentally, when is it 'sexual' and when is it 'harassment'. 'A bit of lark' or 'just a bit of fun' can be experienced as anything but 'a laugh' by the victim. Harassment can be verbal and/or physical. If physical, when does a 'casual touch' turn into a physical/sexual intrusion? Different national and organizational cultures accept physical contact in social encounters to a greater or lesser degree; and it may be hard for some people to interpret the cues of appropriate intimacy. Although sexual harassment is now more openly debated, its stigma and sensitivity are still such that it is likely that a large number of people, women and men, suffer in silence.

Three stories uncover some of the complexities and dilemmas of sexual harassment. The first two accounts, by Susanna (a Chinese student from Hong Kong) and Jason, take us to the heart of the social and psychological processes of sexual harassment. In the third account, from Claire, we get a glimpse of the way a large organization can respond, and how it can backfire.

Susanna's Story: Old Friends?

My name is Susanna Chung. During my first placement I was working for a service company in Hong Kong which is called Transglobe Holdings Ltd. The company is mainly concerned with the provision of services for ships abroad entering Hong Kong. In other words, it acts as a shipping agent.

At the beginning, my boss was helpful and polite. He assigned me to a variety of jobs in different departments. Although some of them were quite mundane with not much responsibility, I learned quite a lot. Thus, I was pleased about it and I greatly appreciated his kindness.

As we spent more time working together, the status gap between us seemed to get smaller. He started to act in a less formal way. He talked to me more frequently than before. But unlike before, the conversations were no longer specifically related to my work. Nevertheless, I thought it was only an indication of our improving friendship, which I saw as a good thing.

Then things suddenly got worse. He gave me less responsibility and treated me more impolitely. He started to talk to me in a different way. For example, he said I should wear tighter and shorter skirts. Also, he acted differently, such as putting his hand on my shoulder while he talked to me. He would ask me to go into his office to see him for unimportant matters, and he behaved in a way which made me feel very embarrassed.

I felt so disappointed. The worst happened shortly before I left the company. He asked me explicitly to have a candle-lit dinner with him so that I would get a brilliant report. My anger exploded because I felt I was being insulted. By that time I could not restrain myself any more. So I replied, 'No way!' Then I walked out of the door and went straight to the toilet and just cried for nearly a hour.

Why could he abuse his authority in this way? I got the job through a friend. My boss, in fact, was her uncle. My friend asked him to offer me a job, even though there were no vacant positions at the time. So I got it because of connections, not on my ability. For this reason, he might have thought he could abuse his authority. He also knew it was unlikely that I would complain about his manners to my friend since it would put her in a difficult position. He paid my salary and now wanted something in return. He was enjoying his exclusive privilege and tried to control me. I believe that if my position in his company had been a more important one, then his behaviour towards me would be very much more restrained.

My boss's behaviour took me totally by surprise. I was utterly shocked by his behaviour as my senior. How could I ever believe that my best friend's uncle would treat me in this way? In fact, we had known each other for quite a time. My friend introduced me to him on one occasion, and he made a very positive impression on me. So I felt very glad and lucky that I could work for him. If anything, I thought his friendship with me would mean that he would treat me particularly well. However, I was wrong. Therefore, I should also be responsible for what happened since I did not protect myself. I should have been aware of what could happen. I encouraged his confidence.

Now, I have learnt a big lesson. Do not trust anybody before enough information is obtained; and don't be misled by first impressions, they can be very wrong.

This tale, told delicately by Susanna, contains many of the dynamics which are central to the way sexual harassment can arise in an organization. There is abuse of trust, status and power, followed by feelings of guilt experienced by the harassed person.

We see Susanna progressively entrapped by her boss, quite puzzled by the shifts in the quality of her relationship with him. She unquestionably accepted his authority at face value, reinforced by her gratitude to him for getting her the job, and as a legacy of an old friendship. She also had a certain deference towards superiors – characteristic of Hong Kong Chinese society.

Her boss, probably sensing this trust, and very aware of her vulnerability and junior status, had another agenda. He gradually turned away from the role of boss supporting a subordinate, to one where Susanna was treated as a sexual object – to be seduced. His conversations and demands became more intimate, his power was used to gain Susanna's attention and to touch her physically. Emotionally, Susanna *felt* harassed, speechless with anxiety, confusion and feelings of affront. Her privacy had been invaded and she had no weapons with which to defend herself. The final attempted seduction was a bribe. The 'dinner' was a thinly disguised offer of the sort: 'sleep with me and I'll make sure you'll be well rewarded at work'. Again, the man's power was being used in a exploitative way.

Susanna ended up turning some of her anger in on herself. She felt that some of the responsibility for the event was hers. This was a very harsh self-judgement, suggesting much-injured pride. It is akin to an innocent pedestrian blaming him or herself for being mugged in the street. Susanna's harassment had little to do with her, and it is an academic point that it might not have happened if she was of a higher grade in the organization (although that could well have been the case). Her boss knowingly exploited her, and herein lies the tyranny of some organizational relationships – especially when power is held in very few hands and there are no mechanisms which an oppressed person can use to be heard. Susanna, a temporary employee, did, in the end, rebel. But that response is sometimes not open to people who cannot afford to risk their boss's displeasure.

Jason's Story: 'Everyone Has Got a Price'

It was the last day of my placement at ZRS Financial Securities in London. We got together in a local pub. As it turned out, it was an establishment where fit female dancers displayed their most private parts for money.

   Out of the blue, my manager asked me: ·

*'Jason what would you have done if you had the choice of either
   giving me a blow-job or being shot by Iraqi terrorists?'*
'I would probably have been dead by now', I answered.

He smiled and asked one of the supervisors the same question. The supervisor would prefer the blow-job. My manager then said to me: 'Jason, never ever forget that everyone's got a price!'
   I was deeply shaken. Although this lunch-hour incident may have been influenced by the environment in which it took place, it summarized to a considerable extent my overall image of the organization. In ZRS they do not pay you for having a good time; they pay you to do a job for whatever it takes (creates an instrumental attitude towards work). The ZRS management is obsessed with the notion that a high enough reward will attract individuals who will thrive in this kind of environment.
   The power of money is incredible in the organization, and the management is to some extent influenced by it. ZRS is officially a success story which thrived in the 80s and is expected to thrive in the future. Personal tragedies of ZRS's employees, such as drug addiction, excessive drinking, cardio-vascular diseases and broken families caused by stress do not make the headlines in the same way as ZRS's quarterly profit figure.

Jason's snapshot of his farewell, and of the organization, is a stark one. In the sexualized atmosphere of a pub, his manager metaphorically exposes himself: a sexual proposition which was very nearly an invitation; a naked expression of power disguised as a piece of worldly wisdom.

Again, the powerful exploit the less powerful. The manager could get away with his outburst, taking little heed of the sensibilities of the student. Anyhow, the student was about to leave so the manager could indulge his own fantasies with little fear of rebuke.

Can Jason's story be a one-off incident, the unguarded behaviour of a 'kinky' manager? Or does it reflect a deeper organizational reality? Jason clearly opts for the latter view, seeing the incident as typical of an organization which believes that everyone can be bought – at a price – to serve it. The human costs are not counted; given what the organization is willing to pay, people do not count beyond doing their jobs. Jason attempted to interpret his manager's behaviour as more than just an outrageous insult. Indeed, maybe Jason needed to do this in order to cope with a very disturbing personal event. But in so doing he opens a window on an organization that views its employees as prostitutes – 'every person has his or her price' therefore 'you will do everything and anything we ask of you because we've paid your price'. This is the breeding ground for exploitation and harassment.

Claire relates the final story, drawn from her experiences working for a large, international chemicals manufacturer.

Claire's Story: Bureaucratizing Harassment

When I was working in Chemsil I witnessed this event. The company had a very traditional culture, yet employed a substantial percentage of women and prided itself upon a friendly working environment. Cultures between the Head Office and factories varied considerably and there were also slight differences between Head Office departments.

The department where I was working had one of the most open, friendly environments. Several young employees socialized frequently outside the workplace, and thus a jovial atmosphere and bear-hugs were not uncommon! However, this atmosphere was to be fundamentally altered by the events following an incident of sexual harassment at the factory site 500 miles away.

One of the line-operators had 'for a laugh' on the day shift removed his trousers and put his penis in a woman's ear, as she sat labelling products, 'to give her a thrill' (could Freud explain this deviance?!). Due to the nature of the incident, the press, local and national, had a field-day. The headlines caused considerable anxiety to the company's public relations department.

In a knee-jerk reaction, in order to be perceived to be acting, the organization immediately announced that every employee was to receive sexual harassment training at all sites (this amounted to several thousand employees). Management consultants specializing in dealing with sexual harassment were called to formulate and implement new policies, and sexual harassment officers were to be appointed. The totally unnecessary scale of reaction caused the organization to become neurotic, paranoid about the possible recurrence of such an incident. All employees had a day off work to have the sexual harassment policies explained, and then be quizzed about them. Employees were told in no uncertain terms what sexual harassment was, and what action would be taken immediately if it did occur. We were each counselled for half an hour:

'Has anyone sexually harassed you?'
'No.'
'Do you understand what sexual harassment is?'
'Yes.'
'And no one has sexually harassed you?'
'No.'
'Has anyone touched you, brushed against you, looked at you, stared at you, sexually propositioned you?'

You could see where this was headed . . . Was I to answer that my boss had put his hand on my shoulder as he leaned above me to get something from the office shelf that I could not reach? That a colleague had accidentally bumped into me at the coffee machine (obviously qualifying as more than a brush)? That everyone in the office had looked at me as I had walked in that morning? That my secretary had stared at my new blouse in admiration, and that I had my usual lunch-time invitation from two of the male graduate trainees asking if I was going to go with them for a lunchtime orgy? And I had replied that I would and I'd put my suspenders and stilettos on!

'No', I replied. Normally I would have joked and shared the banter of a fairly normal office day. However, an anxious feeling stopped me replying. With the prevailing paranoia, my jokes could be taken as a literal account of events, and sexual meanings attached.

For the rest of the week people were quizzed and the environment changed dramatically.

The most noticeable change was in male behaviour, which avoided any physical contact. Even the slightest accidental brush would result in them leaping away, followed by a gushing apology. People avoided eye contact, especially across gender. All office tasks were left asunder as people gossiped about who had said what about whom. Everyone became fearful and suspicious.

A secretary wondered whether she should have told them about a young male trainee who had innocently asked her for a drink after work. The trainee discovered, through the informal network, that she was thinking in this way. He came and yelled at her: did she want him to lose his job? She cried hysterically back that she did not think it was harassment, but now she was not so sure. He grabbed her arms asking her to please stop raising her voice. A senior manager walked in. 'What do you think you are doing to her?' He let go. She said, 'Nothing happened'. 'That's not what it looked like'. He was suspended.

Claire looked at her organization with a mixture of whimsy and despair. Her office, which once enjoyed friendly physical contact between colleagues, was transformed, in a short period, to a place of suspicion, stiffness and careful separation between the sexes. What had gone wrong? Had the organization overreacted?

For a start, Claire reveals little of the probable humiliation and embarrassment of the sexually-harassed woman in the factory '500 miles away', whose story was in the newspapers. How had she been helped by the massive organizational response? Further humiliation?

What was clear was that bulldozing an 'awareness' programme through the organization had four probable consequences – three intended, one unplanned. The first was to mitigate current embarrassment among senior executives. The poor publicity jeopardized the company's image, especially if that image may have suggested they were an enlightened corporation. Secondly, it would counteract implications of managerial indifference; executives could now point to the awareness programme as a positive response. Thirdly, the programme aimed to raise aware-ness among employees about harassment. Those who had never considered sexual harassment as an issue, or who might be unwitting perpetrators, were now flooded with a new conscious-ness. It would be difficult to avoid.

But the fourth – unintended – consequence was a freezing of

interpersonal relationships. People were now nervous, unsure of the interpersonal boundaries they used to take for granted, and fearful of the new managerial controls. What was once felt comfortable and acceptable in face-to-face encounters was now in a possible danger zone. Top management's anxiety had per-meated throughout the organization. Suspicion replaced easy mutual acceptance. In this sense, the attempt to manage the boundaries of sexual encounter had backfired.

There is a fine line to be drawn between an organizational response that offers help and support for the sexually harassed and one that instigates structures that supposedly obviate it. Swing too far to the latter and it, too, can become a tyranny. Criticisms of this sort have been made of other programmes, such as 'race awareness exercises', although all such procedures tread on ideologically sensitive ground and will invariably stir up latent passions. A key consideration for management is how best to include messages about sexual harassment (and other major issues concerning human respect) in the overall style of the organization's culture – from joining the company, onwards. In this way a crisis-response (often becoming an over-the-top response) may be avoided.

Organizations are not sex-free zones. We carry our sexuality into our work – sometimes well repressed, sometimes indirectly expressed, often within the daily banter of work relationships. But what we have shown in this chapter is the dark side of sexuality, as it turns into harassment and exploitation. It continues to go on and it is likely that official statistics represent only the tip of the iceberg.

There are two general considerations to bear in mind. First, a person with an unhappy or inadequate sex life can seek an outlet at work. The drive can be strong enough to cross the taboos of 'proper' working relationships, and power-props that do not exist out of work can be harnessed in work. In other words, the work setting provides some people with the opportunity to do sexually what they cannot achieve outside of work, and with some impunity. If the organization considers it has 'bought' the whole person, then there is an internal justification to exploit – of which sexual harassment can be a part.

The second point concerns the fact that many men and women spend more time in work organizations, between the ages of 18 and 65, than anywhere else. It is, therefore, not surprising that sexual activities such as office affairs take place. It is also, perhaps, not surprising that some people will express their sexual stresses, angers or frustrations on people who appear to be 'easy targets' – less powerful women or men.

How might all this be managed? One of the stories draws attention to anti-harassment training, which is most relevant if integrated into an all-round personnel induction and training process. In some countries there is also recourse to the law for people who have suffered sexual harassment. But such measures have yet to remove the pain, stigma and secrecy associated with sexual harassment. Clearly, both school and management education have important parts to play, not only in raising the subject as worthy of special attention, but also to teach people: (a) the moral and ethical features of the way power and responsibility should be exercised in an organization; (b) management practices which help obviate harassment of all kinds; and (c) organizational structures which assist people safely to express their concerns.

Thinking On

1   Should all sexuality be repressed in work organizations? Would this be the only way of eliminating harassment?
2   Is there too much emphasis on sexual harassment? Could it be just a moral panic or a fad?
3   Have you ever felt sexually harassed by someone, but failed to challenge it? Why?
4   Where do *you* draw the line between sexual harassment and non-harassment?
5   What should be an organization's responsibility for tackling sexual harassment, and what should be the responsibility of the rest of society (e.g. parents, schools, universities, the legal system)?

Reading On

The area of sexuality at work has only recently become part of academic study. The work of Hearn and Parkin (1987) and Hearn et al. (1989) is especially relevant in exploring the contexts and social construction of sexuality at work. These authors criticize previous analyses of organizations (most of which are by male authors) for not acknowledging gender issues. Hearn et al. speak of sexuality as associated with the 'politics of the body' and the negotiated expectations between the genders. Sexuality is embedded in the pattern of emotions and language of the organization. Who gets heard, and why, is explored by Tannen (1995).

Gardner (1995) also develops a number of similar themes, but more broadly in various social settings. Sexual harassment, and its link to power and gender, is discussed by Gutek (1985). Harassment can include offensive language, sexist jokes and negative stereotypes, and frequently plays on the power differences between the harasser and the harassed. Collins and Blodgett (1981) offer an everyday business perspective, while the different national-cultural and perceptual issues are explored by Brant and Too (1994). Important here is how different cultures — and groups within those cultures — define appropriate sexual display, reminding us of the cultural relativity of sexual, and other, organizational behaviours. Sims et al. (1993) have produced one of the few textbooks devoting a full chapter to the issue of sexuality at the workplace; it addresses sex talk, office romances, harassment and the link between sex and organizational politics.

Brant, C. and Too, L. (1994). *Rethinking Sexual Harassment*. London: Pluto Press.

Collins, E. and Blodgett, T.B. (1981). 'Sexual harassment: some see it, some won't', *Harvard Business Review*, March–April, 76–94.

Gardner, C.B. (1995). *Passing By: Gender and Public Harassment*. Berkeley, CA: University of California Press.

Gutek, B.A. (1985). *Sex and the Workplace: Impact of Sexual Behavior and Harassment on Women, Men and Organizations*. San Francisco, CA: Jossey-Bass.

Hearn, J. and Parkin, W. (1987). *'Sex' at 'Work': The Power and Paradox of Organization Sexuality*. Brighton: Wheatsheaf.

Hearn, J., Sheppard, D.L., Tancred-Sheriff, P. and Burrell, G. (Eds) (1989). *The Sexuality of Organization*. London: Sage.

Sims, D., Fineman, S. and Gabriel, Y. (1993). *Organizing and Organizations: An Introduction*. London: Sage.

Tannen, D. (1995). *Talking from 9 to 5*. London: Virago.

15

Surviving

In their recruitment literature, most organizations present glossy images to their new employees and managerial trainees. Smart offices, high technology equipment, challenging work and supportive management are almost always in the picture. What is rarely shown is that many people, even in 'good' jobs, find that their actual work can be very stressful or boring, and that surviving – or simply getting through the day – is what preoccupies them. Handling the negative emotions of being at work constitutes the core of such experiences.

This raises questions about the way organizations set expectations for their employees. How well are job requirements matched with people's skills and abilities? How can organizations respond to employees' distress and meet their needs? Do senior managers want to respond to these needs; are they able to? Do they care about these issues? Should they?

David, Dan and Lim reveal some features of this problem. We begin with David's graphic account of the boredom he experienced. Dan then shows us how his share dealing organization mechanically responded to someone's temporary nervous breakdown. Lastly, Lim takes us with her as she relives the stresses of giving a lecture at a major international oil company.

David's Story: 'The Long Spreadsheet-ridden Day'

By the age of 22 I thought I had done my fair share of boring activities. I thought I knew what boredom was. On the fifth of July, however, they moved the goalposts. This was the day I began my placement with the finance department of Zentor Securities.

All previous conceptions of boredom pale into insignificance. This was boredom lovingly distilled, then distilled again, to a globular mass of pure concentrated boredom. Not wishing to spend too long on the dreary details of the wide array of mind-numbingly tedious roles I was asked to perform, one task in particular illustrates perfectly my role at Zentor: the construction of 'mapping tables'. This exacting and demanding process involved my reading a five-digit number from one seemingly endless list, cross-referencing it with another seemingly endless list (not in numerical order) where the same number may, or may not, have been present next to a code word of twenty-five characters or less. Finally, I would input this number and letter sequence into an Excel spreadsheet. I was required to perform this one particular job, a job that would have sent a white laboratory mouse of only average intelligence stir-crazy within a week, for two months!

As you might imagine, during this time at Zentor I developed, through absolute necessity, quite a range of techniques to cope with the tedium and drudgery. To begin with I did the 'norm' of telling myself that this was my first placement, that everybody had to start somewhere, and that if I worked hard and completed these less challenging tasks with distinction, then I was sure to be rewarded with something more worthwhile to do. However, after a couple of months with no change and with no prospect of any change in the future, the benefits of this technique soon wore thin.

My primary method of coping with the nine-to-five drudgery of a job I hated was to make sure that most of the time during the day which was mine was still my own. This began in the morning with ensuring that I always read a novel on the way to work on the tube. I saw this firstly as my way of using the hour each day travelling as mine, rather the company's time, and secondly as a means of provoking thought and ideas within myself that I might consider during the long spreadsheet-ridden day that stretched before me.

The desire to make most of the time my own time next manifested itself in my lunch hour. Here I would strive to prolong and enjoy the hour as much as possible by getting as far away from the office as possible, both mentally and physically. This took the form of going for walks, going shopping or even just going to a different place for lunch; anything to mark the time as my own. This behaviour was, however, most prevalent when I returned home in the evening, when, despite any degree of tiredness, I felt driven to go out in a desperate attempt to delay tomorrow's return to work just a little bit longer. I felt this compulsion to such a frightening degree that I would frequently experience quite violent mood swings, ranging from depression to panic, if I was unable to orchestrate sufficient evening diversions to prevent me from even thinking about the next day's work.

It is difficult for me to assess how successful I was in coping with my boredom and lack of fulfilment at Zentor. I can only say that, given its effect on my morale and state of mind, just to complete six months was, I feel, success enough.

Could I have handled the situation differently? On careful consideration I feel I can safely say that I explored every single means of improving the value of my placement. However efficiently and enthusiastically I completed each mundane task set, it would only be replaced by more of the same. Furthermore, my requests to my manager for some more taxing and varied work were ignored. Then eventually, when my requests turned to complaints, I was treated with nothing but contempt. There is no way I would put myself through such a demeaning, alienating and unrewarding experience again.

It is not uncommon for a company to give the least-challenging work to its junior staff. If that person is also temporary, like David, then they can sometimes justify this to themselves. But the other side of the equation is that students such as David are bright, can offer creative energy to challenging jobs, and will have a low boredom-threshold for routine work. The company, ostensibly, is interested in recruiting the Davids of the world when they graduate, and are also keen that the students take away a good impression of the company. Clearly, something had gone radically wrong in the Zentor Securities case.

David was thrown back on psychological coping mechanisms to fight off the numbing tedium of his work. It is noteworthy that his coping style did not simply switch off when he left work. He somehow had to recover his composure in compensatory activities, and felt panicky if he had nothing structured. Like much of work-life, it interacts with non-work activities, and the balance is not always an easy one to maintain. If a person is used like a machine at work, it is likely that the human and emotional costs will eventually show. David knew he would leave after six months, so he stuck it out. Permanent employees, dependent on the income they earn from the job, have far less choice. Arguably, 'mapping tables' should have been done by a machine, or not at all; or perhaps by someone more at ease with highly routine mental work.

David was at a loss to know how to change his circumstances, especially after his appeals to his manager had been rejected. He felt no natural justice, or reward for his efforts. He assumed (as many people do) that hard work and doing well at a boring job will earn something more worth while. He did not have the power to alter his situation, so he retreated. He became very possessive of 'his' time, a pattern noticeable in other people who have jobs which they find intrinsically boring or meaningless (e.g. they leave on the dot of 5 p.m., or put the telephone down on a customer because it is the end of their working day).

We do not know why his manager did not respond, but it requires time, care, and attention within the managerial process for a work placement to operate effectively. It is not untypical for one central department of a large corporation to accept a student for internship, and, when the student arrives, for another operational department to be asked to 'find them some work'. The actual commitment to the student's welfare can be low, or perhaps justified as a rite of passage necessary for all newcomers – 'we all had to do the boring work when we started'.

Dan's Story: Papering Over the Cracks

I started talking to a chap that I had seen around in the office, but had not actually had the opportunity to speak to before. Our conversation revolved around financial careers in the City. He told me of the massive employee turnover in the company and the City in general. Of the sixty or so people working on the floor at the time he first joined Targets, the stockbrokers, five years ago, only five are still there now. Since then, enough people have passed through the company to fill the place three times (approx. 1200 people). One person who worked in his department had just been head-hunted by another City institution with the offer of an undisclosed six-figure salary.

This then led on to a rather hushed-up story of an incident concerning one of the senior brokers upstairs, Ray (reputedly earning £250k basic per annum), that happened over the Christmas/New Year period. Ray, incidentally, had been in trouble a few years ago because he disclosed details of his salary to a national magazine. That contravenes company policy.

Well, it had been an unusually bad day bond-trading. Ray, clearly under a great deal of work-related stress, 'cracked'. He then went berserk. He vented his frustration firstly by smashing many of the PC screens on his floor. Then, in the company car park (reserved for senior employees and directors), he repeatedly drove his Porsche into the wall, severely damaging several cars in the process. Finally he burst into a leaving party on the second floor, with the apparent intention of assaulting the member of staff for whom the party was being held. At this point he was apprehended by security staff.

The company's reaction to this incident was simply to unofficially suspend him for a week, and request a written apology. He resumed his position a number of days later.

This story had quite an impact on me. The City may be rife with nepotism but it is still essentially meritocratic. Clearly the management considered that it was more viable to repair the physical damage caused, than to lose the massive revenues gained through Ray's trading. The incident was contained and did no damage to the company's public image. Had he been dismissed he would have undoubtedly received offers from other competing firms within the City (possibly taking a proportion of his client base with him).

Here, the management's priorities were to protect the profitability of the organization and to ensure the greatest chance of survival in such a cut-throat environment. In this line of business, company loyalty is low, as demonstrated by the massive staff turnover. Employees tend to be particularly self-interested and are working for themselves rather than for the benefit of the company, and it was clear to me that there was a degree of resentment towards Ray. This individual approach to the work led to a surprising amount of bickering and back-stabbing outside office hours. They are motivated mainly by the excitement and challenges of working in a high stress environment, the potential salaries and the social status of their job.

Youth appears to be a prerequisite, in order to cope with the extreme stress levels, and the incredibly long working hours. Many people may only last up to ten years in the industry before they 'burn out'. As is perhaps illustrated in the above incident, the job takes over your life.

At the time I was quite stunned by the conversation – amazed and angry at the way someone could behave in such a way and actually get away with it. At the same time other, more expendable, employees could be dismissed for relatively minor offences. However, looking at it now from the company's point of view, I realize that while such an incident is hardly excusable, the management reacted in the only way possible considering the importance of the member of staff involved.

Where David's story points to the crippling effects of low-demand work, Dan's account shows that living constantly on the edge, under the pressure of high demands, can cripple in a different way. The dealing-room floor is notorious for its casualties alongside the thrills, excitement and (sometimes) huge financial rewards. What is intriguing about Dan's story is the way the organization managed to contain the 'incident' and retain the services of the derailed dealer. There are two keys to understanding this – secrecy and status.

In many organizations the public antics of a distraught employee threaten its existing social order; it embarrasses management and risks bad publicity. Often the organization's first response is to care for itself rather than for the employee. The 'sick' employee is retired early, put into a less-exposed role or, if there is damage of the sort evident in the present case, dismissed for 'unprofessional' or criminal behaviour. But the culture of the stock market dealing room is different. We see immediate damage-limitation and a conspiracy of silence; a normalization, or business-as-usual response. Ray is away for just a week. Yet Ray was no small cog in a big wheel. Normally he performed very well and his loss, in revenue terms, would hurt the organization economically. He may have been a bit unpopular, and unstable, but was not as expendable as other employees. His offence, although gross by most standards, was therefore smoothed over and officially forgotten.

The dealing room is an atypical organization, where the combination of self-interest, high pressure and ruthlessness is extreme. However, it is sobering to note that Dan, in his final paragraph, began to take on board the organizational reasoning. Caring for Ray's personal sanity was not mentioned, and Dan accepted justice skewed in Ray's favour – if it preserved the financial interests of the organization. The nicer points of ethical conduct may soon be submerged in the depersonalization of organizational activities.

Lim's Story: Baptism of Fire

The big occasion; a formal presentation of my research and ideas on future world energy production to an audience of energy experts at OilCo!

Only ten minutes to go before my boss arrives. I could hear myself constantly questioning: Are all my transparencies in order? Have I photocopied enough handouts? But, more importantly, do I look presentable? Black velvet suit, hair tied back, understated make-up, uhm . . . perfect, . . . I hoped!

Why the fuss and the feeling of nausea? Well this was my first opportunity to really show them what I was worth. I would either impress them and receive recognition or be branded as hopeless for the remaining twenty weeks. My objective, the former – naturally.

Ten-thirty a.m. and a tap on the door heralded the entrance of my boss Steve. A quick smile and a nod of the head towards the lift meant that it was time to walk over to the downstream building for my presentation at 10.40 a.m.

On entering the conference room, I was confronted by a mass of tables which were arranged in a square, with the projector at the far end of the room. A sense of panic as I began to realize the importance of the next hour. Again anxieties and questions. How many people were going to come? There must have been seating capacity for at least 50 to 60, but although the room was large it had a comforting feeling, a sort of familiarity.

Oceans of blue and grey suits then proceeded to enter. They seemed to be fairly relaxed, with coffee in one hand, files and paper in the other. There was also the usual hum of chatter dotted with the occasional outburst of laughter. At the front I busied myself by arranging my notes, preparing myself, at which point I noticed that a special seat was reserved for the coordinator head. This seat was positioned fairly near to the front and had quick access to the door.

What seemed like a lifetime of waiting was in fact only a few minutes, before Peter Fallow, the Director, entered the room. All eyes turned towards him in the hope of making eye contact, followed by broad smiles and extended hands. The beginning of the presentation was marked by his step towards his chair. My onlookers followed and seated themselves one-by-one, positioning themselves near the head man.

A brief introduction was made by my boss but then it was up to me. The next forty minutes 'just happened'. I heard my own voice echoing around the room but it was their body language that said everything. Arms were folded, heads tilted, chins were rubbed, and eyebrows furrowed. I was being watched.

I cleared my throat, took a deep breath, and smiled a smile as if to apologize for my pathetic existence. My every move was being scrutinized. Me under a microscope! Swarms of eyes were fixed on me and with a mixture of curiosity, bemusement and wariness.

Shakily I placed my first slide up and began. I knew my material inside out, so I was on autopilot.

During the presentation I had a demoralizing feeling that managers have a reluctance to give any praise or feedback. I interpreted it as failure. Later, however, I realized that new ideas were absorbed slowly, and the time it took them to ask questions meant that I had sufficiently inspired them to think. This was a recognition of success by everyone.

Approval was a significant factor as I was one of only three females among thirty-five men, at least half their age and of a different culture to myself. I was a representation of a somewhat unknown, and therefore threatening, group. Some positive gesture or comment from any one manager secured a certain amount of respect, but when it did come it came from Fallow, which meant I had passed the test and could enjoy the security of acceptance.

Significantly, Fallow had a pink seat instead of the normal green, and the higher job-grouped managers got to sit closer to him, not by plan but automatically. Everyone knew their place despite the informal layout of the room. This also illustrates the ingrained hierarchical mentality; they have a surprising amount of respect for their seniors and often look up for direction. All these points epitomize the inconsistency between what is portrayed in the literature supplied by the public relations department, and how it actually operates. Inside one feels part of a hierarchy although the company is supposedly operated under a matrix system.

Survival in some organizational settings is tied intimately to one's presentation of self at a single point in time. You have to 'get it right', to prove yourself by passing successfully through an 'ordeal'. There are not always precise rules to follow, so improvisation is essential. Lim's self-examination is a sensitive reading of her own behaviour and feelings of vulnerability during such an ordeal. It reveals not only the minutiae of her experiences during her crucial lecture, but it also holds up a mirror to the organization – its pecking order and status cliques. Unlike Ray in the previous story, Lim had not acquired a reputation for indispensability and high performance.

With pounding heart and churning stomach, Lim attends beforehand to the presentational devices she thinks will be important: personal appearance, visual aids, positioning on stage, facial expression – striving to get them right. She is on stage, but in a very unfamiliar, unpracticed, role. What should she say? How will the audience react? The precise composition and size of audience are unknown; she has to assess them as she goes along, so the risks of a poor performance are considerable. In counterpoint, the audience are a bit uncomfortable, unsure of what to expect from the drama about to unfold. What should they look for? What should they applaud? After all, Lim is not an established manager; she is also female and Chinese.

In the stress of being watched by many people, her reputation at stake, it is hard for Lim accurately to interpret the audience's reactions. She cannot be sure she is doing the right thing. In her subsequent reflections, Lim stumbled on a key turning point. The organization only masqueraded as a relatively egalitarian one. The actual hierarchy was ever-present, powerfully symbolized by the chair-colour and layout in the audience. Once the top-boss was pleased, everyone started to be pleased; a signal from the chief and everyone else fell into line.

The cliché 'we all learn from experience' contains some important grains of truth in survival circumstances. So audience silence is not necessarily bad news for the presenter, and knowing key 'targets' in the audience can help. Over time and with practice, one's improvisational repertoire increases in breadth and skill, and confidence improves. It becomes harder to be caught off balance and easier to shift from one perspective to another. Other than in highly routine activities, it is improvisational skills – the abilities to pull off a good act and think on one's feet – that set apart the more effective survivors. And such skills can rarely be learned from books.

Thinking On

1   Have you been afflicted by boredom in a job at work or an extremely tedious school task? What have you done to survive? How could changes in the way the work was organized help?
2   How do you think people survive jobs for many years which, in your view, must be very tedious to do?
3   Is Dan right that the dealing-room organization did the appropriate thing in keeping Ray at his post? What should we do about the person who is clearly not surviving?
4   What examples are there of people who clearly fail to improvise appropriately in their public performances? What exactly goes wrong? (Consider politicians, for a start.)

Reading On

All the stories highlight facets of the role expectations and demands of organizational life, especially the pressures and stresses from work underload or overload. The accounts are not unlike some of the stories of work graphically portrayed by Studs Terkel (1975). These indicate how jobs can be stultifying, a threat to self-image and personal competence. Cooper (1994) and Luthans (1992) outline some of the relevant stress theory in this area. These works are a part of a huge publication output on stress – a psychological variable, seen to be caused by an interaction of personality and organizational/situational factors. This literature offers ways of conceptualizing stress, the effects of role underload, overload, ambiguity and conflict (e.g. Kahn et al. 1964; Cooper 1991), and different ways of managing, or coping with, stress. This last area includes personal, therapeutic techniques and changes to the structure of the organization. Stress theorists tend to agree that understanding individual differences in the appraisal of situations is very important, as one person's sense of challenge can be another's overwhelming burden. Recently stress has been linked more broadly to our understanding of emotions at work (Lazarus 1993; Fineman 1993).

Conventional perspectives on stress have come under radical attack by Newton et al. (1995). Is stress necessarily an inevitable fact of modern life, an individual's own disease and responsibility? Who defines whom as stressed? Stress should be seen as an emotional product of the social and political/power feature of organizational life, not an individual's 'weakness'. Is it, perhaps, too convenient for managers to label stressed workers as suitable cases for treatment? Managers are less able or willing to question the structure and ideology of managerial and corporate expectations which contribute to the problem. This is sometimes called blaming the victim.

For readers interested in the pressures and peculiarities of the dealing-room experience, Kahn and Cooper's (1993) study is a helpful one. The stories in this chapter, in different ways, also point to the politics of organizational life – who is favoured, who is to be pleased, who can be ignored. Pfeffer's (1992) writings are illuminating in this sphere.

Cooper, C.L. (1991). 'Stress in organizations', in M. Smith (ed.), *Analysing Organizational Behaviour*. Houndsmills, Basingstoke: Macmillan.
Cooper, C.L. (1994). *Creating Healthy Work Organizations*. Chichester: Wiley.
Fineman, S. (ed.) (1993). *Emotion in Organizations*. London: Sage.
Kahn, H. and Cooper, C. (1993). *Stress in the Dealing Room*. London: Routledge.
Kahn, R.L., Wolfe, D.M., Quinn, R.P., Snoek, J.D. and Rosenthal, R.A. (1964). *Organizational Stress: Studies in Role Conflict and Ambiguity*. New York: Wiley.

Lazarus, R.S. (1993). 'From psychological stress to the emotions', *Annual Review of Psychology*, 44, 1–21.

Luthans, F. (1992). *Organizational Behavior*. New York: McGraw-Hill.

Newton, T., Handy, J. and Fineman, S. (1995). *'Managing' Stress: Emotion and Power at Work*. London: Sage.

Pfeffer, J. (1992). *Managing with Power*. Boston, MA: Harvard Business School Press.

Terkel, S. (1975). *Working*. Harmondsworth: Penguin.

Final Thoughts

This is a book of stories – stories which chronicle life in organizations, seen through the enquiring eyes of our students. Like any book of stories, our book stands or falls by whether readers find the material interesting, amusing, moving, alarming; in short, whether it resonates with their own experiences and interests.

We found these stories rich, diverse and full of the kind of detail of organizational life which often goes unreported in conventional books. Our commentary has drawn your attention to some of these features, some themes and some contrasts. We have resisted the temptation of over-elaborating on the meanings that the stories held for us. Over-interpreting a story, like explaining a joke or dissecting a play, can kill it; it is a sign of a good story that it will evoke different feelings and different meanings in each person. There is no reason why readers should not reflect on individual accounts, examine what their own reactions might have been had they held the role of the central character in the tale, and unravel what made the situation important for the storyteller.

The accounts in this book were not chosen for any reason other than they each seemed meaningful and interesting to us. We had not planned to group the chapters of this book in three parts, yet as we started to reflect on the material, the three broad themes – *images and reality, winning and losing, injuries and survival* – seemed virtually to recommend themselves. It can be said that these large themes reflect the preoccupations of young people about to embark upon careers in business.

The composite picture of organizations which emerges from these accounts is rather dark. This may be due in part, as suggested earlier, to the storytellers' disappointed idealism or premature cynicism; but we feel that it also says something about the harsher, turbulent realities of organizational life which they encountered. At the turn of the twentieth century, ruthless competitiveness, uncertainty, arbitrariness and moral confusion seemed to be becoming endemic in many organizations. While management rhetoric was extolling quality, teamwork and the value of the human resource, the lives of many in organizations became precarious, selfish and unpredictable. Reputations and careers were rapidly made and even more rapidly fell to pieces. Defensiveness, suspicion, fear and contempt discoloured relations between people. These are all characteristics of times of turbulent social change, of an era which will bring about a shake up of social norms, standards and expectations.

How useful are the stories as windows into the organizations themselves? Clearly, no claim can be made either about the factual accuracy of any one of them or about the extent to which an incident is typical of the organization as a whole, beyond the student's assurances to that effect. Yet, in reading and reflecting on the reports, we envisaged a test of validity which, in our view, most of them would pass. If we were senior managers or directors in the company from which a story emanated, would we find something practically useful, something to think about or work on, in terms of our own managerial aims and objectives? Do the stories tell us something about our organization which, *prima facie*, would be worthy of further enquiry and possible action?

It seems to us that the stories contain much useful material in this sense. They are unusually frank expressions of real experience which, as managers, we would worry about – or even find rather shocking. How well are we employing these bright, young people? Are we misleading them? Are we allowing them to experience important rewards soon enough? Are their stories revealing aspects of decline or arthritis in our organization that we cannot, or will not, see? How might we reverse this? Are we allowing cliques of powerful people to run the place, under the guise of democracy? What of our equal opportunities policy – is it really a sham? Do we have a meaningful and effective human resource management policy? An even more uncomfortable thing to ask – are we, personally, the main part of the problem?

We leave the closing words to one of our students:

Having your illusions shattered is a thought-provoking experience. And seeing such internal conflict on my second day, working for a company I thought I knew, definitely changed the way I then went on to interact with people within the company. What had I been taught? That the problem with so many large organizations is the bureaucratic red tape that shadows anything anyone attempts to do. As I sat in the conference room, surrounded by portraits of board members, my mind returned to lecture halls and tedious theories of organizational structure. To say that theory had turned into reality may seem to be a gross cliché but I remember feeling how ironic the situation was and how well it fitted into everything I had learnt.

Index